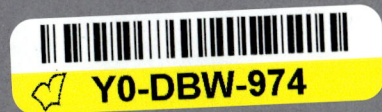

THE LEGENDS OF
MOTORSPORT

Dave Friedman, August, 1992

1423/2550

THE LEGENDS OF
MOTORSPORT

ISBN 0-9632751-0-0

Dedication

To all of the people who helped make this period of racing so special.

Table of Contents

Acknowledgements

This book is very special to me and I've had a lot of help from a number of outstanding people who made it happen.

The book never could have happened without Ernie Nagamatsu, who believed in the project, when no one else would. I have been blessed with the best creative staff that anyone could have wanted to work with: DeWitt Frasier, Maggie Logan, Nancy Nagamatsu, and Carol Isago are responsible for the look and production of this book. They put quality first: something which seems to be a dying art in this day and age. Michael McEvoy (Mario Andretti), David Mills (Derek Bell), and Andrew Hampel and Clare Collinson (Jackie Stewart) were very helpful in scheduling time to obtain these signatures. (Maggie Logan also contributed in many other ways, particularly in making the driver's signature process much less complicated.)

Other people who have contributed to this project are: Dick Wallen who made me never lose faith; Phil Harms whose wonderful USAC statistics helped me identify drivers in 30 year old photos; Michael Jordan and his excellent editorial skills, and Kathy Weida and Evi Gurney of All American Racers. Dick Wallen also provided, from his vast collection, the photograph of A. J. Shepard's dirt car crash on page 318.

Several people were most helpful in helping me promote this book. Art Eastman of Vintage Motorsport Magazine, Lynn Mills of Vintage Voice Magazine, David Treffer of Maryland Motorsports Gallery, Kevin Blick of Car Classics and Mick Walsh of Classic and Sportscar, and Jacque Vaucher of l'Art et l'Automobile Gallery offered advice, promotion and advertising space. To them, a huge thank you.

My deepest thanks to my friends Dan Gurney, Nigel Roebuck, John Surtees, and Eoin Young for taking time away from their busy schedules to share their marvelous memories, at the beginning of this book.

Finally, I can't say enough about the 22 Legends of Motorsport who took time from their busy schedules to sign our special limited editions. Chris Amon, Mario Andretti, Derek Bell, Jack Brabham, Vic Elford, George Follmer, Dan Gurney, Jim Hall, Charlie Hayes, Phil Hill, David Hobbs, Denis Hulme, Jacky Ickx, Innes Ireland, Parnelli Jones, Stirling Moss, Lothar Motschenbacher, Brian Redman, Jody Scheckter, Jackie Stewart, John Surtees, and Rodger Ward exemplify the true meaning of the word professional. They are the reason that racing was, is, and always will be such a great sport.

Dan Gurney, United States Grand Prix, Oct. 4, 1964

Dave Friedman has his shop just across the street from All American Racers, so I see him pretty often. Every week during the production of this book, he has brought me a few photographs to look at, and every week I am surprised at how many races he attended during the time when I was driving. It's almost as if Dave and his camera were there for all the big days during my career.

It's all a long time ago, of course. Someone came up to me at this year's 12 hours of Sebring, which our AAR Eagle-Toyota won for the first time, and he asked me for my autograph and then asked when it was that I actually stopped driving race cars. I told him that I officially retired in 1970. He looked shocked and said, "But that was years ago. How come you're still famous?" I just laughed, and, really, I can't explain it myself. I guess racing was just different in those days, so we remember it more. And when I look at Dave Friedman's photographs it reminds me just how different it was.

I remember the first time I raced a Formula 1 car, the Ferrari 246. It was at Rheims for the 1959 French Grand Prix, and I remember that Ferrari had rented a garage that was maybe five miles from the track. The way they got the cars to the track was to tell the drivers to just drive them on the street. It was the most fabulous thing. You're going through a regular city with a full-on Grand Prix car with not a hint of a muffler or anything and you can spin the tires anytime you want. The people are waving and yelling, and you're gassing the dickens out of this thing, and it was just fabulous. You can't imagine the thrill of being able to drive a car like that on the local roads. At the traffic lights, the people are yelling and there's nobody to tell you that you shouldn't be doing that, and the police themselves are waving you on. Oh, it was just great, let me tell you.

Of course, some of the racing from years ago was just the same as it is now. Maybe the cars now seem pretty crude to us, but at the time we were experimenting with the latest technology — high-rpm engines, wide tires, stiff chassis, aerodynamics, all of that. And I was with the acknowledged masters of that moment in the history of racing technology every day of the month.

When I think about those days, I also think about the genie getting out of the bottle, because money became more and more important in the 1960's. Of course, we weren't amateurs. Racing is a form of war, and if you are going to fight a war successfully, you had better have lots of resources. We were asking the same questions we do now: why does something feel the way it does?, what makes one car faster than another? Each time you ask these questions, it costs money to take the blindfold off. So we learned pretty quick that if you get left behind in the money race...boy, that's tough. So sponsorship and prize money were just as important to us then as they are now.

In the end, what I appreciate most about Dave Friedman's photographs are the faces of the people I raced against. We saw each other a lot in those days because we raced everything — formula cars, Indy cars, sports cars, and even sedans. And we saw each other in the paddock a lot, too, because we were all down in the dirt, working on our cars and trying to make them run faster.

There are a lot of faces that I remember. Skip Hudson, my first friend in racing. Phil Hill, my Ferrari teammate who proved to the Europeans that Americans were fast. Tony Brooks, also my teammate at Ferrari, who was one of the greatest natural talents I've ever seen. Graham Hill, my BRM teammate, who had such a wild sense of humor. Jack Brabham, who always kids me about leaving his Formula 1 team just in time to help make him World Champion in 1966. John Surtees, who accomplished so much in cars and on motorcycles. Parnelli Jones, who used to broadcast intimidation just by walking around (heck, he's still that way). My friend Jerry Grant who turned the first 200 mph lap in one of our Eagles at Ontario. Pedro Rodriguez, who almost never had a car that was as good as he was. Jochen Rindt, who I introduced to the Indy 500. And of course Jimmy Clark, who was as great a friend as he was a racer.

There are a lot of people I remember from those days, too many that have been a long time gone. This book brings a lot of them back.

Dan Gurney
April, 1992

V

Bill Bryce, Bruce McLaren, Jim Clark, Phil Hill, and Eoin Young enjoy some good times during the 1965 Tasman Series in New Zealand.

Legends are memories of heroes. Heroes are special people, so Dave Friedman's album becomes a collection of memories of special people. As we all have our own memories, the photographs become multi-faceted, showing different sides to different people, each reader seeing something the other has missed, a special personal angle that escapes everyone else. The book becomes an intensely personal record of racing history. Friedman reminds me of racing writer Denis Jenkinson. Both can look like a pair of unmade beds but their talent transcends their appearance. Where Jenks can write things about racing that others dare not even think about, Friedman's special ability with a camera has produced flashes of genius. A shot of cars or people that you feel couldn't or wouldn't have happened but there in Friedman's photograph, a captured square of racing history.

Dave Friedman enjoyed the luxury of being there when racing history was being made; those exciting years that spanned the 1960's and 1970's when drivers and car-makers discovered there was more to speed than excitement. Drivers became engineers and then champions. Friedman followed the fortunes of Carroll Shelby and his Cobras while Bruce McLaren gave me the chance to be in on the formation of his team and to be around when his mighty CanAm cars were being dreamed of

and then built and raced. To be honest it didn't seem like history being made then, it was more like work. Not work in a 9-to-5 sort of way—well, not the way I did it!—but a means of being paid for what you would have paid to do. The drivers thought that way in those days too. Now it's all changed and being paid more than the multi-millionaire beside you on the grid has become another side to racing. Fortunately this professional side of racing has changed the game so much that it has offered a historical cut-off point which is pretty much where Friedman ends his book. I like to think of it as my period also so I'm delighted that he offered me the chance to indulge in this forward.

Bruce McLaren gave me my chance to get into racing when he asked if I would be his secretary in 1962. I asked what a secretary did and he said he didn't really know but most of the other drivers had one, so I could be his. Being a mate of Bruce's rather than a journalist opened doors everywhere and I could rate drivers like Jimmy Clark and Phil Hill as friends around the tracks when incidents happened that seemed funny at the time but became hilarious after being told over a hundred dinner tables down the years. For instance, the time Phil was arrested in New Zealand on the Tasman Series. An American tourist had been robbed of $20 in travellers checks and Phil had gone to the bank

that morning to change $20 in travellers checks! We waited lunch for him in the quiet hotel off the town square and when he finally burst through the double doors, he stunned the other diners, mainly country farmers in town with their wives, into silence when he said "Where have I been!?, I've been in JAIL is where I've been!" He had been picked up on the pavement outside the bank and bundled into a squad car. At one point the driver leaned 'round and asked one of the other cops who he was. "He SAYS he's Phil Hill the racing driver," came his colleague's reply. One cop remarked pointedly on Phil's expensive wrist watch and Phil told him he had been presented with it after winning Le Mans. So it would be engraved? Of Course. Phil unbuckled the watch—and there wasn't a mark on the back! Which came, perhaps, from winning Le Mans on too many occasions.

Bruce McLaren won Le Mans only once but he and Phil had become firm friends; Phil the last of the front-engined Ferrari brigade and Bruce one of the first of the rear-engined Cooper drivers. After Bruce's death in 1970 I wrote a book in tribute to his career and in the re-telling of the Le Mans years with Ford I mentioned the story about Dan Gurney and A. J. Foyt deciding to "do a clutch job" on their car rather than soldier on around the clock but the big Ford held together and they won. This was probably an apocryphal tale, an adaptation of what really took place that has passed into legend — that work again — but Dan took exception to seeing it in print 20 years ago. "I never said that," he growled. "And if I had said it, I wouldn't have said it to HIM…" Dan always seemed to be an eternal college student with an easy grin and what I suppose now was a Californian way of being in Europe. Richie Ginther was the same. Laid back. I remember John Cooper saying that we had reached the end of the road with race car development when Colin Chapman introduced the monocoque Lotus 25 in 1962. The engineer in Ginther was incensed and we sat down to write a feature in which he talked about Grand Prix cars with automatic transmission and wings. Pretty heady stuff then but part of the technical scene now. Old hat almost.

I first met Jim Clark when I was standing in pouring rain up to my ankles in water on a soaked infield of the Wigram Airfield Circuit and Jimmy was spinning his Lotus down towards us in walls of water. It was one of those rooted-to-the-spot scenes from a bad dream. Whichever way we ran he would have spun into us so we instinctively stood still. Instinctively, nothing. We were just scared stiff and COULDN'T move! He stopped, stalled, a few feet away. The spin had probably lasted a quarter of a mile. We tried to push-start him but the rear

wheels just locked and the tires just skidded on the wet grass. He suggested that we should push him out onto the tarmac of the straight itself and push again there.

Those cars that were still on the track and racing were blasting through a few feet away, unsighted in the spray. We said that, on balance, we didn't think we would. So he took his helmet off, shook hands with a bunch of soaked Kiwis and we all walked back across the airfield to the pits chatting with the man who would win World Championships and the Indy 500 and become one of the greatest racing drivers in history. You couldn't have met people like that by making an appointment…

I was lucky to be a New Zealander when they were thick on the ground in Grand Prix racing. Bruce was creating his little empire from a tiny team in an incredibly dirty trading estate near Heathrow Airport. It seemed like a 10,000 sq. ft. palace to us then because we had come from an even dirtier shed that we had shared with a huge road grader. That was where the sleek little Zerex Special, the Cooper-based sports car that Roger Penske used as his launch-pad to fortune and fame, was transformed into the brutally ugly Cooper-Oldsmobile with its stack-pipe exhausts. The chassis was finished on a Sunday and we had forgotten to buy paint. Sunday in Britain in those days was very much the Sabbath

and all the shops were shut, with the exception of a little garden shop where I bought the only tin of paint they had, a soft green for garden gates and shed doors. That first of the line McLaren sports car was known as the Jolly Green Giant because it was the only paint I could find. I rode around Europe with Denny Hulme in 1961 when he was racing a Formula Junior Cooper in remote events in France, Italy, Denmark, Sweden — wherever he could get an entry. One weekend we went to Monza to be told that Hulme hadn't entered. In fact he had entered for the race at Rheims, the curtain-raiser to the Grand Prix, so we drove through the night and arrived in the race city bleary-eyed at dawn to try and find a room. We booked into a flea-pit hotel and as we were coming out of the room on race morning, we noticed that our neighbour locking his door was wearing Dunlop blue overalls. I asked Denny who it was. "Dunno, never laid eyes on him." It was Giancarlo Baghetti, who would become the first rookie to win a world championship Grand Prix that afternoon. As a second-string newcomer with Ferrari he had been allocated a flea-pit hotel for his brief weekend of glory.

Bruce was bliss to work with, looking back on it. After each race we would tape his column, which was syndicated to various magazines and there were times when he had come back from a long-haul flight that he would take the tape into the bath and you could hear the bathwater gurgling and McLaren giggling as he remembered something else he wanted to put in his column. At a Goodwood test session in 1966 he offered me a ride 'round the track in the prototype M6 CanAm car. This powerful two-seater offered the unique opportunity for people like myself to see how people like him performed at rather closer quarters than usual. We rumbled around for a lap and he shouted across to ask if I was OK. I was fine. A bit uncomfortable crammed in there, but beginning to think that being a racing driver wasn't quite as difficult as I had imagined.

The second lap was a bit faster, but I was wondering how I could ask Bruce if I could have a go. He shouted across again to ask if I was OK. I gave a confident thumbs-up, and then he booted it. The world went into a blur and my memories of the next few laps became a snatch-bag of disjointed flashes, as the storming acceleration glued you into the back of the seat and the giant's-grasp braking hurling you forward into the instrument panel, while all the while the G-forces of cornering were shipping your body this way and that. Woodcote corner at the end of the long straight looked as though it had been loaded in a cannon and fired straight at you. There was no way we could survive this speed so far into the corner before he was on the

brakes and into it and then blasting away to the next assault on your senses. Mercifully he eventually backed off and we cruised into the pit and a return to sanity. It was the first and last time I ever entertained thoughts of being a racing driver...

Chris Amon was chaos out of the car and an artist in it. He was only 19 when he drove in his first Formula 1 race and he would become regarded as one of the pure talents in racing but fate stopped him winning on a string of occasions. His business world was a succession of managers and a career of failed opportunities, but Chris was fun to be around. He shared a house with Peter Revson, Mike Hailwood, Tony Maggs and others and they were known as The Ditton Road Fliers after the road they lived in. Their parties on weekends between races were not to be missed. We were just ending an era when drivers drank and Amon and Hailwood were the last of a line of party people who could lead the singing late into the night, and line up on the grid for a spirited race the next day. It was an era that couldn't last but it was great to have been part of it. At least it provides a yardstick with which to judge the drivers of today.

Jackie Stewart loves to tell the story about the time he offered me ten percent of everything he earned if I would be his manager. It must have taken me all of ten seconds to weigh up the proposi-

tion and reject it. After all, I was working for a Grand Prix driver and this little Scotsman was only in Formula 3. If you're going to do it, do it BIG. That includes mistakes because then people remember them and you can talk about them over dinner thirty years later and make them sound like reasoned career decisions. Mark Donohue made overtures about me being his manager at one time when he took me aside and asked what the Formula 1 drivers were being paid. I told him and he was very quiet for a while and then told me what he was being paid by Penske. Did I think I could act on his behalf and ask Roger for more money? It was another of those ten-second decisions that has resulted in Roger still talking to me. There has never seemed to be a time to tell him about all the money I saved him by not going in to bat for Mark.

This has become something of a personal saunter down memory lane, but I suppose if you were bored you would have stopped reading by now. Hell, I've enjoyed it. It reminds me of where I've been all these years. Dave Friedman's photographs? They will too. An artist remembering his art. Enjoy.

Eoin Young
January, 1992

John Surtees, United States Grand Prix, Oct. 6, 1968

The period covered by this book was a particularly exciting and eventful one for me. My first Formula Junior Race had been in 1960, followed by a Formula 2 race and then into Formula 1 with a works Lotus 18, that is, when I could fit it in around what was to be my final year of Grand Prix motorcycle racing. 1960 was to be the last year of the old 2½ litre Formula. We were to see the birth and demise of the intercontinental class, where Tony Vandervell's rear engine car appeared for the only race of the Series that was held, with yours truly driving, at Silverstone. The new 1½ litre safety-inspired Formula arrived in 1961, only to be replaced by the 3 litre Formula for 1966.

Events in my life during this period included gaining the World Championship in 1964, my divorce from Ferrari in mid-season 1966, winning the first Can-Am Championship in 1966, the joining with Honda for 1967-68, the building of the successful F5000 cars to be followed in 1970 by the first Surtees Formula 1 car and our winning of the F2 European Championship with Mike Hailwood in 1972.

It was a period where Grand Prix drivers, the likes of Jimmy Clark, Graham Hill and Dan Gurney enjoyed driving a Formula 1 car one weekend, a Formula 2 the next, a saloon car, a sports prototype, or an Indy car.

It was all deadly serious and highly competitive. It was very much less commercialized, which of course meant that far lesser rewards in pure monetary terms were available than today. However, levels of enjoyment, satisfaction and motivation in getting it right I am sure are not exceeded today.

We all drove on some fabulous circuits before many of them were turned into guard-railed tunnels, and the high speed straights, sweeps and turns all had a chicane cut in them. You still met the men who actually designed the cars and made the parts. You would have two mechanics per car. The total personnel of a team like Ferrari would amount to perhaps 15 people at a race. Yes, it was very different.

I recall when I first met Dave Friedman, it was 1963 when my team set off to challenge the American Specials in the North American Sports Car Series, first with a borrowed works prototype Ferrari, stripped of all its surplus long-distance equipment, and then with a Lola T70. The Team consisted of one full time mechanic, who drove the van between venues, a Chevy van and trailer, myself as Team Manager, part-time mechanic and driver, plus a few local North American enthusiasts who could always be relied upon to give a helping hand. Dave Friedman, because of his own bubbling enthusiasm and highly professional use of his specialist skills, has captured some of the very best of the racing scene. A racing scene which touches upon the many people I feel privileged today to look upon as friends, competitors and past associates in what, to us at least, was a very special period.

John Surtees
March, 1992

Nigel Roebuck with 3 time World Champion Jackie Stewart.

Probably Brock Yates put it best; we were ruminating one evening about how racing had changed, nostalgia perhaps liberated by Scotch. Whatever, Yates was in a reflective mood, "Do you ever think," he murmured, "that this sport has out-teched itself?"

I did, and I do. As I write, in the spring of 1992, it seems even Ayrton Senna may be starting to feel the same way. Recently he tested a new McLaren F1 car, complete with "fly-by-wire" technology, and afterwards he said he didn't care for it. Oh, it worked well enough, but somehow it offended the driver in him, the competitive spirit. It was a fundamental part of an individual's style to control the car with what God had given him. But with this system...why, much of the job was done by electronics.

"It will be the same for every driver," Senna remarked. "Keep your foot down, and the rest will be done for you. I wish we could all have a standard system, where you really drive the car. But...this is the modern technology, and you have to follow it if you want to be competitive."

"It was the same with 'active' suspension," Ayrton went on. "Technology making you faster through the turns, faster against the watch. Semi-automatic gearboxes reduced shifting to a single finger movement; 'traction control' systems guaranteed you were catapulted off the grid. And all of these things," he concluded, "took something away from the driver." Inevitably offensive to any man of genius.

Before we fall completely into the "everything was better in the old days" trap, however, we should recall that not everything was. During a recent clear-out of my study, I came across an awful lot of Memorial Service sheets from the sixties and seventies, stark reminders every one of how perilous a sport this once was. Anyone with a detectable IQ must rejoice that now race drivers routinely walk away from accidents unsurvivable even a dozen years ago.

We must thank Technology for that, but as it has given, so also — in my opinion — has it taken away. Stirling Moss once described the perfect racing car as having "slightly more power than the chassis could handle," and I don't believe the magic ingredient of motor racing was ever better defined.

"Towards the end of my career," Stirling says, "I drove a Lotus, which was undoubtedly a better car than the Cooper I'd had before, in the sense that it was more efficient. But I enjoyed the Cooper far more, because it was a car you could overdrive, which was very satisfying. The limits of the Lotus were much higher; it was hard for anyone to look average in a Lotus..."

For me, the abiding problem with contemporary motor racing is that the cars have become too efficient, spawning the delusion one could drive them oneself, given the ability to cling on. I liked to watch an ace out of a corner with just the right amount of opposite lock, imposing his will on the car, driving it a little faster than it cared to go. In the modern era, though, a car sliding is a car losing time.

I have felt passionately about this sport since childhood, but in truth my interest in racing cars has never extended much beyond how they look, how they sound, how they go. I was never much one for science, and saw this thing always as a human activity.

"People don't come to see aerodynamic brilliance, to see cars that look like the driver is bedding in the brakes," said Gilles Villeneuve, as pure a race driver as ever there has been. "They come to be entertained, to see a spectacle. Smoke the tires! Yeah!"

Years ago I wrote a book, *World Champion,* with Mario Andretti. He had recently won his title in a Lotus 79, and spoke with something like reverence of Colin Chapman, the great innovator. Andretti is a man, unchanging in himself, who has ridden with the times, understandably grabbing for any slice of technology which will make him more competitive; to win has always been the thing.

Ask him, though, where he has found most pleasure in motor racing, and Mario will talk not of Indianapolis or Monza, but of the sixties, of Championship racing on a dirt mile. "Nothing else gives the same animal satisfaction you got from pitching one of those things sideways at 130 mph, and holding it there on the throttle. No wings, no tricks, just balance..."

In my dotage, I shall recall that I saw Senna and Prost, the grands seigners of Formula 1 in their time, but also that I sat in Stirling's Maserati 250F when I was a kid, watched Jimmy Clark at Silverstone, Jochen Rindt at Monte Carlo, Ronnie Peterson at Barcelona, A.J. Foyt and Mario at Indianapolis, Gilles at, well, anywhere you care to mention.

I shall remember, too, that to admire the driver was not necessarily to like the man, for the qualities needed for success at the top levels of motor racing—like any other competitive activity—often manifest themselves unattractively out of the car. But an Andretti, a Villeneuve, an Amon, anyone could be proud to have known, and there are many others besides.

Over time I have built up a huge collection of racing memorabilia, books, programmes, posters—and also photographs, many of them taken by Dave Friedman. It is a black art to me, an abiding mystery. I can take pictures of racing cars and people with reasonable competence, but somehow they rarely "live." Friedman's work, like that of all great racing photographers, stands as something apart, something to be savoured.

This book brings back a lot of heroes for me, brilliantly evoking a time in motor racing when a computer was something that filled a fair-sized room, when mechanics fiddled with screwdrivers, and drivers wandered around a garage area with goggles slung around their necks, when a motorhome was also somewhere for a party, and something that was serious could also be fun. Above all, it was a time when a great driver could win with an average car. If I love racing still, and always will, that time stands highest in my affections. Before the sport "out-teched" itself.

Nigel Roebuck

Nigel Roebuck
March, 1992

THE LEGENDS OF MOTORSPORT

Jim Clark, Graham Hill, and John Surtees represent five of the world championships won during the 1960's. These three brilliant drivers are seen enjoying a light moment before the start of the Mexican Grand Prix in November, 1964. John Surtees clinched his only world championship by finishing second in this race. Surtees remembers "It was an honor to know and compete against such men as these."

F O R M U L A   1

I was privileged to have seen, what in my opinion, were the best years of Formula 1. I attended my first Grand Prix race at the U.S.G.P. at Riverside in November, 1960. It was there that I was able to photograph the legendary Stirling Moss winning the final race of the 2.5 Litre Formula in his Rob Walker Lotus 18. It was also great to see Jack Brabham and Bruce McLaren in the Cooper T53s that set the standard for all of the future rear-engine cars and the last of the front-engine grand prix cars, the ill-conceived Reventlow Scarab.

The next five years were devoted to the smaller 1.5 Litre Formula. It was during those years I was able to see Clark, Gurney, Graham Hill, Phil Hill, Surtees, Brabham, and so many other greats drive their incredible tiny machines. I will always remember watching Dan Gurney trying to squeeze himself into the Porsche 804, Jimmy Clark driving the incredible Lotus 25, John Surtees wrapping up the world championship in a *white and blue* Ferrari, and the crude beginnings of the Honda F1 effort. My biggest regret was that I was never able to see Phil Hill drive the shark-nosed Ferrari 156 during his championship season.

The year 1966 brought a new excitement to Formula 1. The 3 Litre Formula was born, and power, speed, and noise returned to the circuits of the world. Exciting new cars such as the Lotus 49-Cosworth, AAR Eagle-Westlake, BRM H16, Repco-Brabham and the Honda V12 appeared and attendance records were broken everywhere. This was an era when the grids were filled with drivers who were all capable of winning, given the proper situation.

By the time I attended my last F1 race in 1983, I had seen all of the great drivers from Moss to Prost, and great advancements in life-saving car safety. I feel fortunate to have seen the era when drivers drove in polo shirts, had no restraining belts, and mingled with each other and the fans who paid to see them race. Above all, I was glad to have seen the time when rides went to the best driver, not the one who just brought the most money. It was a very special time that I will not forget.

Chuck Daigh drives the Scarab in its final Grand Prix appearance at the United States Grand Prix in November, 1960.
Daigh finished tenth in the only race that the Scarab F1 car ever finished.

Bruce McLaren, outfitted in a polo shirt, driving a Cooper T53 in the 1960 United States Grand Prix. In November 1959, at age 22, Bruce McLaren became the youngest driver to win a Grand Prix by winning the United States Grand Prix at Sebring.

Stirling Moss wins the final race of the 2.5 litre formula in Rob Walker's Lotus 18. This was the year that the United States Grand Prix was held at Riverside International Raceway in November, 1960.

In 1960, Jack Brabham won his second consecutive world championship driving a Cooper T53. This car was the forerunner of many of the great rear-engine cars to come.

The Cooper Team sits in the pit area of the 1962 United States Grand Prix. Things were certainly a bit less hectic at that time.

One of racing's most thrilling moments is the start of the race. The start of the 1967 United States Grand Prix has Graham Hill (6), Dan Gurney (11), Jim Clark (5), and Chris Amon (9) in the front two rows.

Ronnie Bucknum spent his first season in Formula 1 sorting out the 1964 Honda RA271. This car was powered by a 1.5 litre V12 engine.

By 1965, Ritchie Ginther joined the team and gave Honda its first victory at the Grand Prix of Mexico. Ginther drove the Honda RA272 which was also powered by the 1.5 litre V12 engine.

By 1967, John Surtees joined the Honda team and gave them one of the most spectacular wins ever. In a Grand Prix race when he beat Jack Brabham by half a car length at the Grand Prix of Italy. Surtees drove a RA300 powered by a 3.0 litre V12 that year.

By 1968, Honda's final season in Formula 1, Surtees was driving the RA301 powered by the 3.0 Litre V12 engine. This car did not allow Surtees to achieve the success of the previous season.

The spartan cockpit of the 1965 Ferrari 12 cylinder Grand Prix car.
Note the rather small fire safety bottle on the far left.

The clean and efficient Team Lotus garage at Watkins Glen in October, 1963.
Quite different from today's massive undertaking.

Colin Chapman caught placing a 1964 *Dan Gurney For President* sticker on one of his Team Lotus'. Can you imagine this happening today, especially when the candidate drives for a rival team?

Pedro Rodriguez, Graham Hill, and Jo Bonnier enjoy Jim Clark's duck hunting technique, while Dan Gurney and Jack Brabham don't see much humor in it.

Graham Hill seems delighted to be presented with a photographic opportunity.

A typical signaling pit of the era. The man with the pit board will get the necessary information from the man with stop watches, barely visible on the right. Note all of the drivers' names on the ground and how some of the abbreviations are spelled.

A humble beginning for an organization that was to dominate the engine development side of modern Grand Prix racing. The first Honda Formula 1 car is parked in the pit lane of the 1964 United States Grand Prix. Note that the tiny 1.5 litre, 12 cylinder engine is mounted vertical to the driver. It was rumored that Honda had taken two of their 6 cylinder motorcycle engines and put them together to form the 12 cylinder power plant.

It's late 1965, and Jack Brabham might be trying to talk Dan Gurney out of starting his own team and staying with Brabham for 1966.

Dan Gurney's finest day in racing came during the 1967 Grand Prix of Belgium when his AAR Eagle-Westlake scored its only Grand Prix win. It was the first and only win ever, for an American driver in a car that he had built and it was also the fastest Grand Prix ever run to that time.

Dan Gurney in the car that gave him his first Grand Prix win at the 1962 Grand Prix of France. The car was the Porsche 804 powered by a 1.5 liter flat eight cylinder engine. This was the only Grand Prix victory for the Porsche team.

Three good friends, Dan Gurney, Jim Clark, and Graham Hill share a moment prior to the start of the United States Grand Prix in October, 1962.

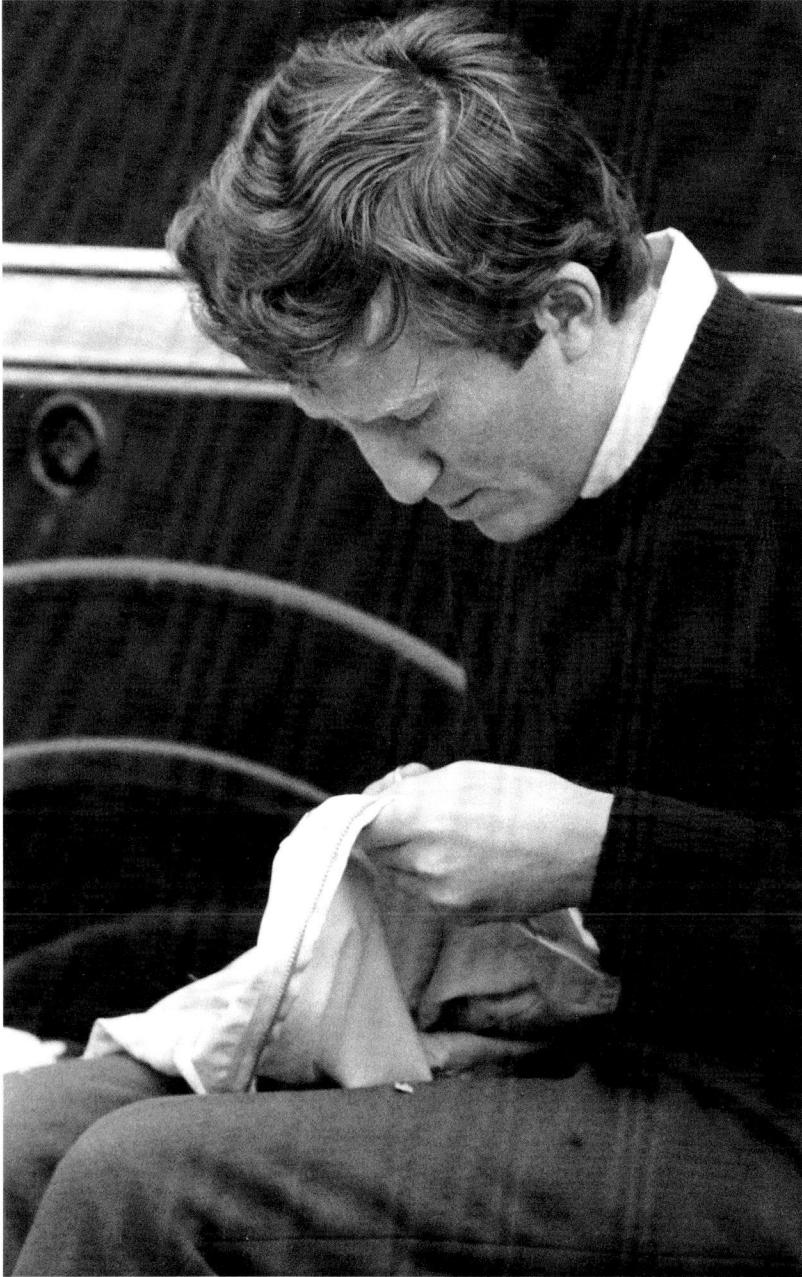

Jochen Rindt demonstrates his new found domestic skills at the
Dutch Grand Prix in June 1967, while...

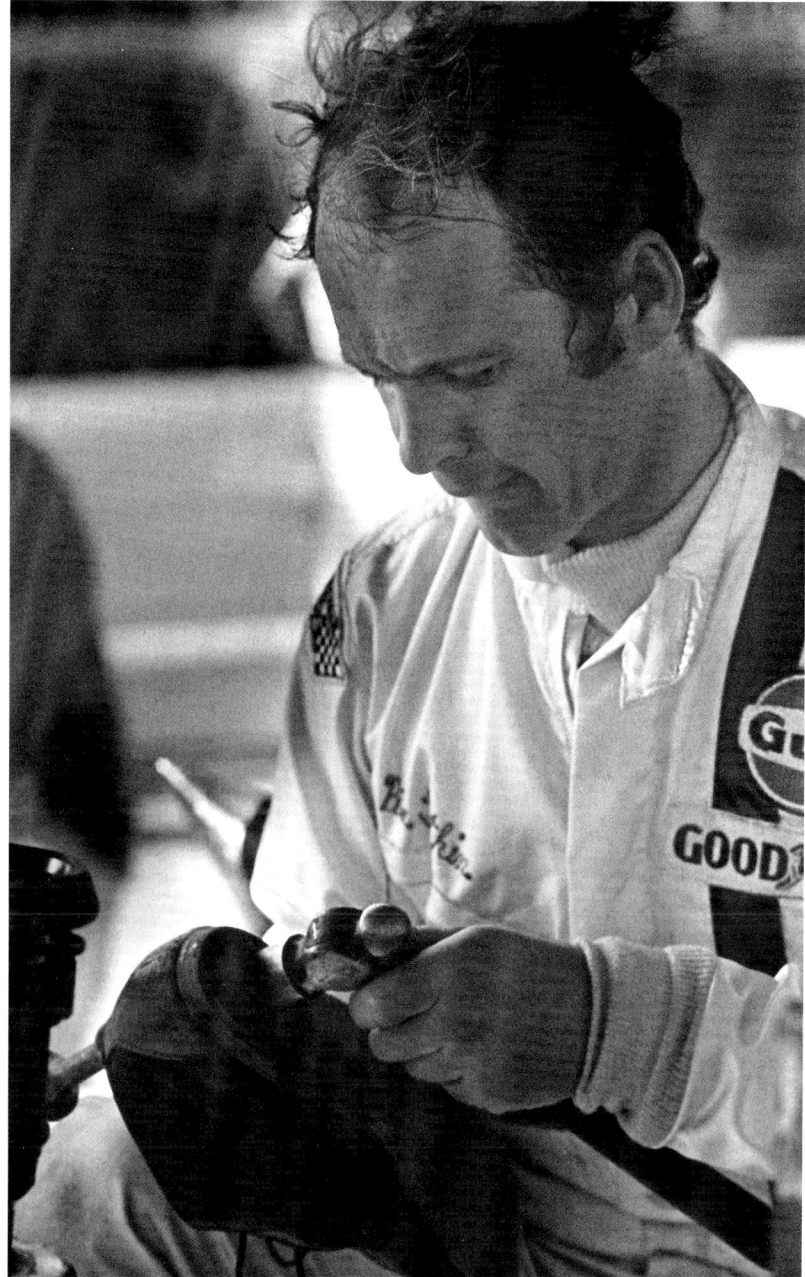

Peter Gethin illustrates his cobbler technique at the
South African Grand Prix in March 1971.

Jim Clark and teammate Mike Spence enjoy lunch while reviewing lap charts with Colin Chapman during practice for the 1965 United States Grand Prix.

Ritchie Ginther, hard at work in the Honda RA273 V12, during the 1966 Grand Prix of Mexico. One year earlier, Ginther gave Honda its first Grand Prix win at this race.

The first Grand Prix car produced by McLaren in 1966 was a far cry from the incredible machines produced by the company today. The McLaren M2B of 1966 was powered by a Ford Indianapolis V8 dual overhead cam engine that was linered down from 4.2 to 3 litres. This package proved to be under powered and was not successful in spite of the talent of drivers Bruce McLaren and Chris Amon.

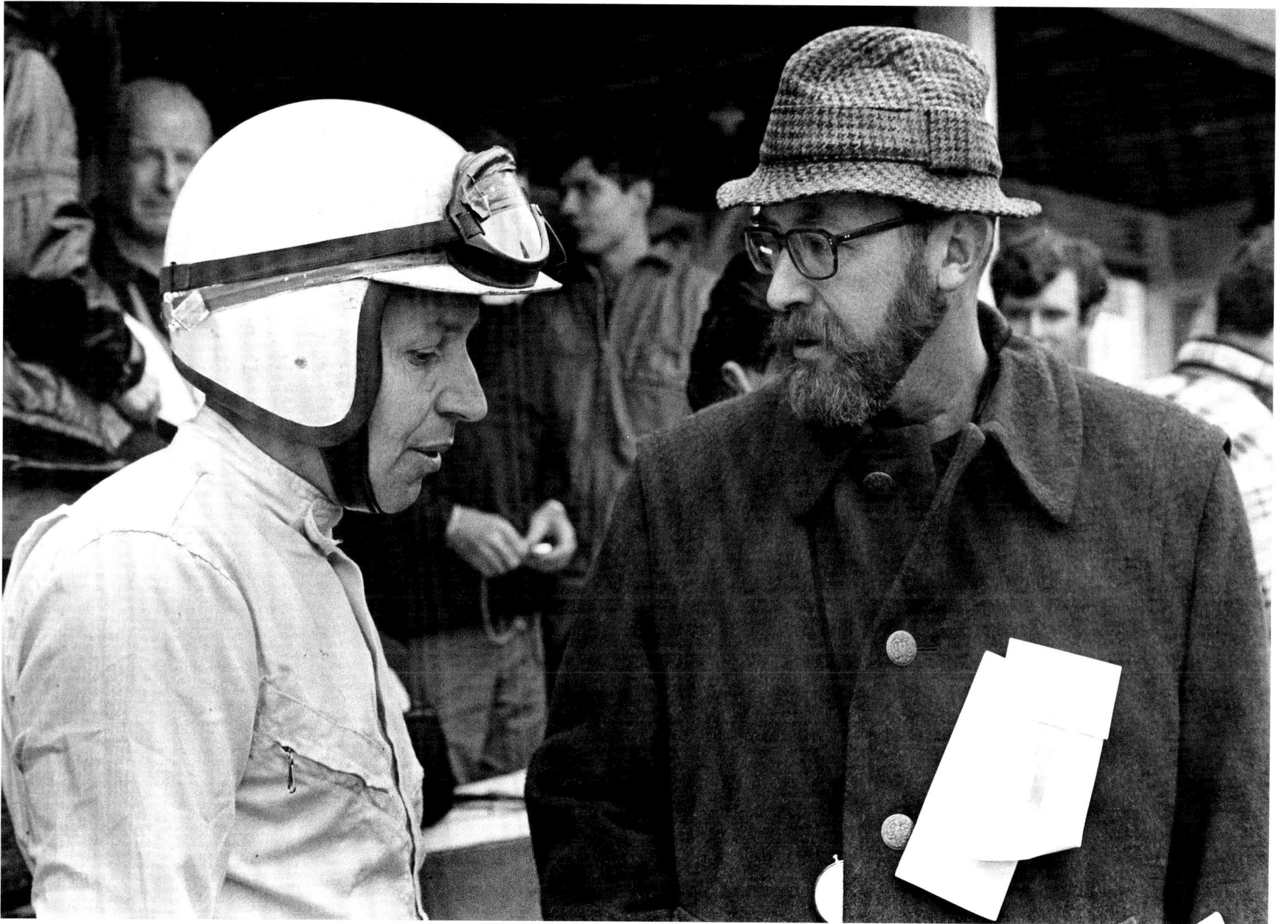

John Surtees talks to well known British journalist Denis Jenkinson during a break in the action at the 1966 United States Grand Prix.

Innes Ireland's BRM is shown leading Bruce McLaren during the 1966 Grand Prix of Mexico. Although Ireland gave Lotus their first Formula 1 win at Goodwood in 1960, he is probably best remembered as one of racing's most legendary characters.

Chris Amon — Ferrari 312 — Grand Prix of Mexico — 1967.

Jackie Stewart — BRM H16 — Grand Prix of Belgium — 1967.

Ronnie Peterson — March 711 — Grand Prix of South Africa — 1971.

Denis Hulme — Repco-Brabham — Grand Prix of Mexico — 1967.

The Gurney-Westlake V12 is warmed up in the pits before the 1966 United States Grand Prix. 1966 was a year of development for the Eagle team, but the Eagle-Westlake would achieve two victories in 1967.

Lorenzo Bandini watches as his Ferrari
mechanics make some final adjustments to
his V12 1.5 litre engine.

The Cooper transporter, seen in the paddock of the 1967 Dutch Grand Prix, was typical of the vehicles used by the teams of the era.

Patty McLaren enjoyed her role as timer and scorer for her husband's team. Usually, the driver's wife or girlfriend handled these chores during the season.

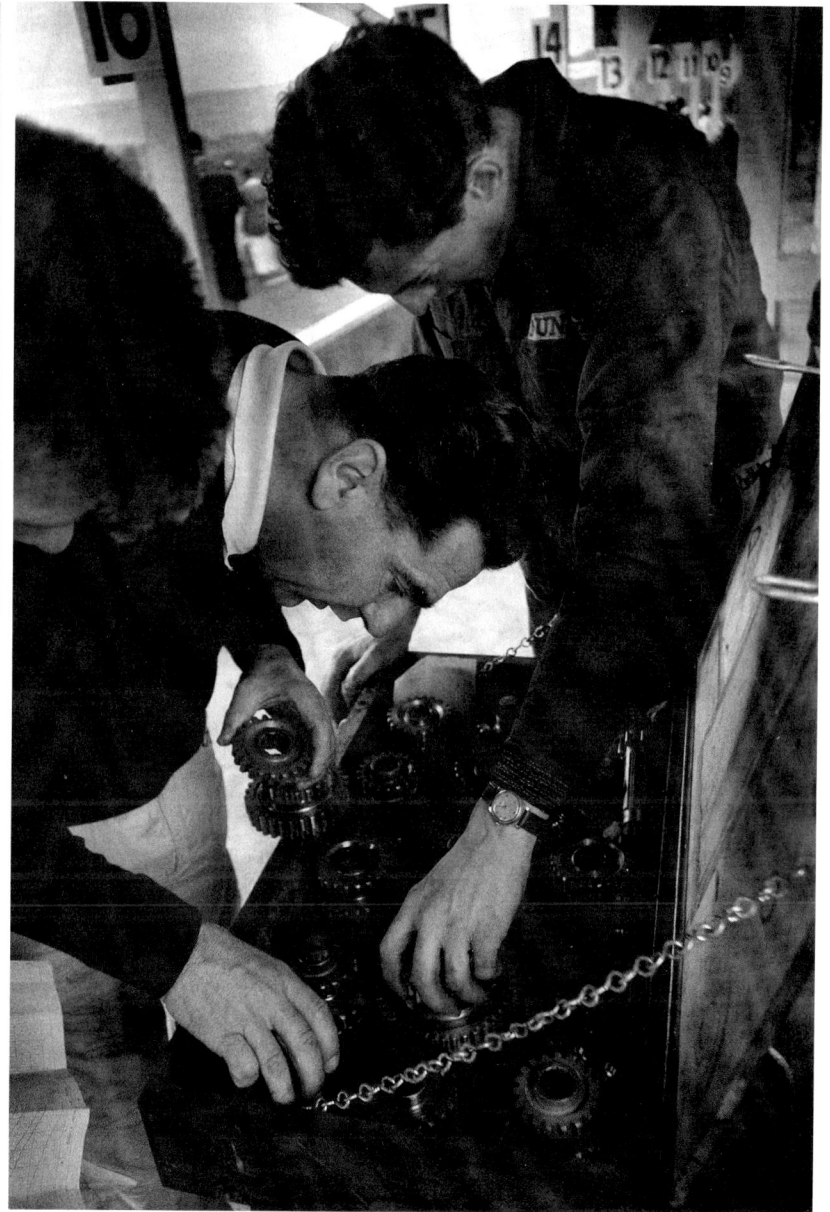

Famed car builder and engineer, John Cooper, selects the proper gears for his 1962 Cooper Climax effort at the United States Grand Prix.

Dan Gurney—USA—1967

Denis Hulme—New Zealand—1967

Vic Elford—England—1968

Jack Brabham—Australia—1967

Bruce McLaren—New Zealand—1967

Jim Clark—Scotland—1967

Chris Amon — New Zealand — 1967

Some loved it, most hated it, but rain was a fact of life on the Grand Prix circuits of the world. Ritchie Ginther, shown here in his BRM at the Grand Prix of Mexico in October, 1963, was one of those who did well in the rain.

The rain provided some close action although those directly behind another car were seldom able to see very well. Jack Brabham (1) in his Repco Brabham, heads for victory at the rain swept Grand Prix of Canada in August, 1967. Bruce McLaren (19) and Jackie Stewart (15) chase Brabham.

Phil Hill in a car he would rather forget. Although designed by ex-Ferrari engineer Carlo Chiti, the ATS was ill-fated and proved to be a disaster.

The interior of the Anglo-American Racers shop in Rye, Sussex, England, June, 1966. There are three Grand Prix Eagle chassis in different states of construction visible here.

The engine that dominated racing for years to come, debuted at the Dutch Grand Prix on June 4, 1967. The Cosworth DFV 8 cylinder engine coupled to Colin Chapman's Lotus 49 chassis, driven by Jim Clark, proved to be a winner in its maiden effort.

Classic Clark. Arms crossed and eyes focused in total concentration on the corner ahead, Jim Clark heads for victory, and his first world championship, in the rain-swept Mexican Grand Prix of October, 1963. Clark won seven of ten Grand Prix races that year in one of the great Grand Prix cars of all time, the radical monocoque Lotus 25.

Colin Chapman and Jim Clark having a serious discussion prior to the start of the United States Grand Prix in October, 1964. Clark and Chapman shared a special relationship throughout their years together from 1960 until Clark's death in April, 1968.

A young Jacky Ickx seeks advice from former driver and Cooper team manager Roy Salvadori. During the 1966-67 seasons, Ickx drove a Cooper-Maserati.

Teammates and good friends, Jim Clark and Graham Hill enjoy one of Hill's witty comments before the running of the Dutch Grand Prix in June, 1967.

Mike Parkes seems to be saying, "Can't you torque it a bit more to the left lads" to his Ferrari mechanics.

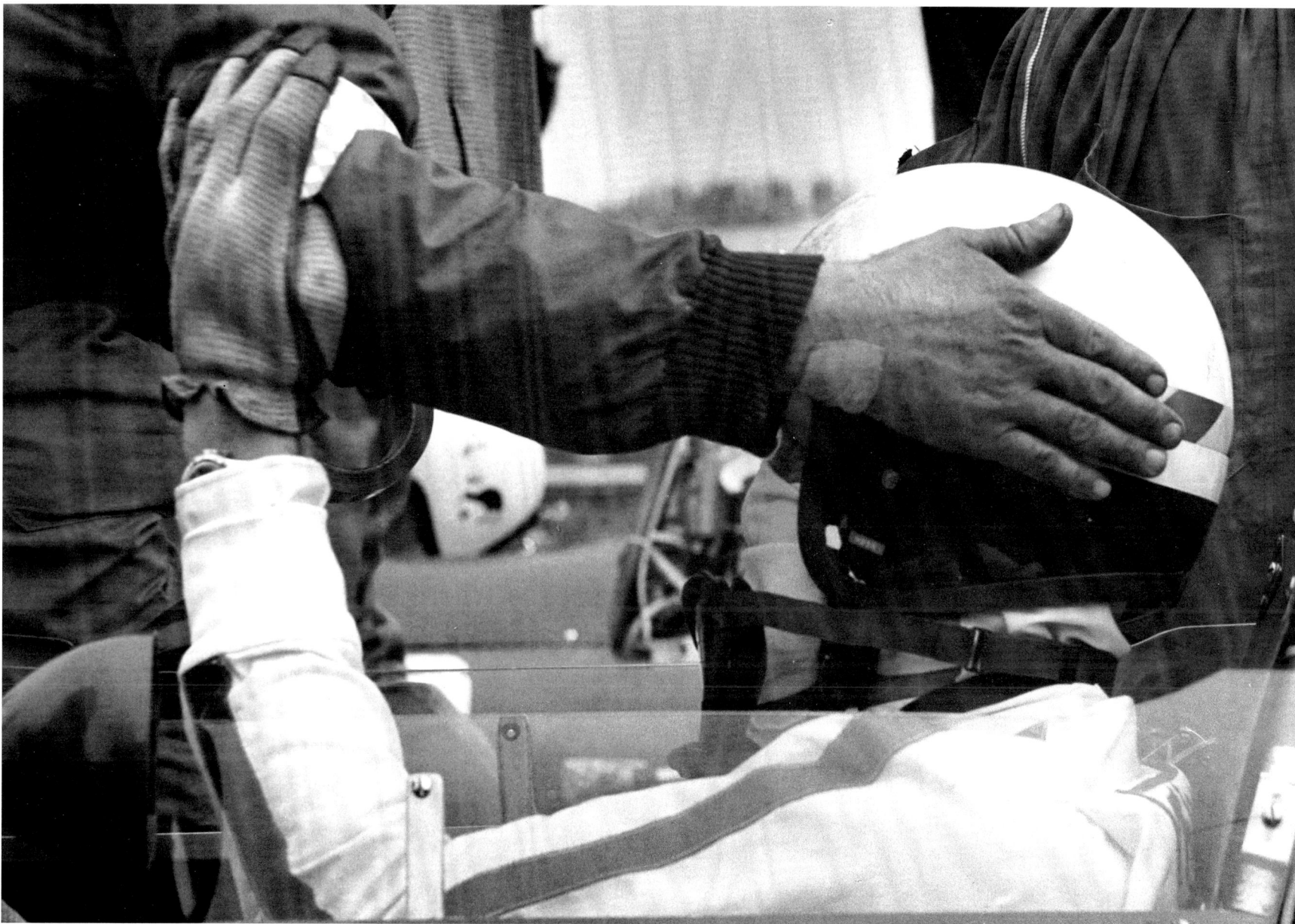

Mike Parkes shares a special moment with his Ferrari mechanic just prior to the start of the 1967 Belgium Grand Prix. Moments after this photo was taken, Parkes was involved in a terrible accident that ended his Formula 1 career.

Jackie Stewart, Chris Irwin, and Mike Spence formed the 1967 team for BRM.

Jack Brabham and long time colleague Ron Tauranac in a serious mood prior to the start of the Dutch Grand Prix in 1967.

A driver's view of the photographers that crowd the grid prior to the start of a grand prix.

Mario Andretti made his grand prix debut a spectacular one by winning the pole position for the 1968 United States Grand Prix in his Lotus 49B. Unfortunately, he failed to finish the race due to clutch problems.

On March 7, 1971, Mario Andretti achieved his first grand prix victory at the South African Grand Prix. Driving a Ferrari 312B, Mario set a new race record for the event.

1968 Indianapolis winner Bobby Unser made his first grand prix start at the United States Grand Prix, in October of that year. Unser, driving a factory BRM, went out of the race with a blown engine.

John Surtees left Ferrari to join the Cooper-Maserati team and gave them their first victory at the Grand Prix of Mexico, October, 1966.

Jim Clark wins the 1967 Dutch Grand Prix and gives the new Lotus 49 powered by the Cosworth V8 engine a victory in its initial race. Denis Hulme, driving the Repco-Brabham #2, went on to win the 1967 world championship.

Graham Hill proudly wears the #1, reflecting the defending world champion, on the side of his BRM during the 1963 season.

Jo Siffert's Cooper-Maserati leads Scarfiotti's Ferrari #22, Spence's BRM #10, and Irwin's BRM during the early laps of the 1967 Dutch Grand Prix.

Jo Siffert, after he drove his BRM to a well
deserved victory at the 1968 British Grand Prix.

Dan Gurney is surrounded by well wishers after his popular win at the 1967 Belgium Grand Prix.

Bruce McLaren, sportcoat and all, in deep
concentration before the start of the United States
Grand Prix in October, 1968.

After two years of frustration, the McLaren team finally scored their first three Grand Prix victories during the 1968 season. Fittingly enough, Bruce won the first race in the M7A at the Belgium Grand Prix on June 9, 1968.

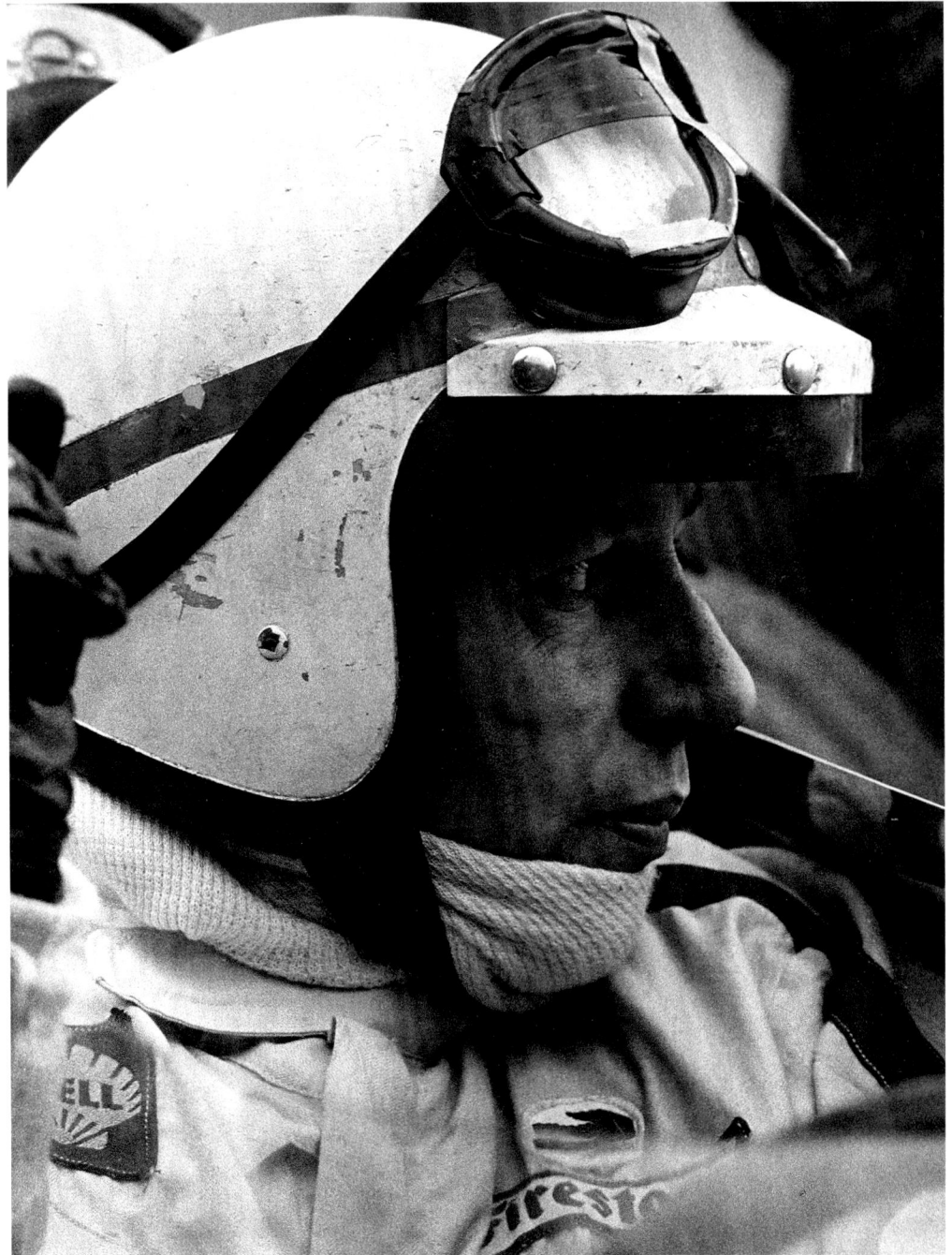

John Surtees, World Champion, 1964. Surtees is the only man to ever win World Championships on both two wheels and four, having won 7 World Motorcycle Championships for M.V. Agusta before turning to cars.

Graham Hill, World Champion 1962 and 1968.

Ferrari Technical Director Mauro Forghieri with three of his best drivers of the era. Here with Mike Parkes, Ferrari's top test and development driver at the Dutch Grand Prix in June, 1967.

Chris Amon, Ferrari's number one driver during the 1967 season.

And Lorenzo Bandini, Ferrari team driver at the United States Grand Prix in October, 1964.

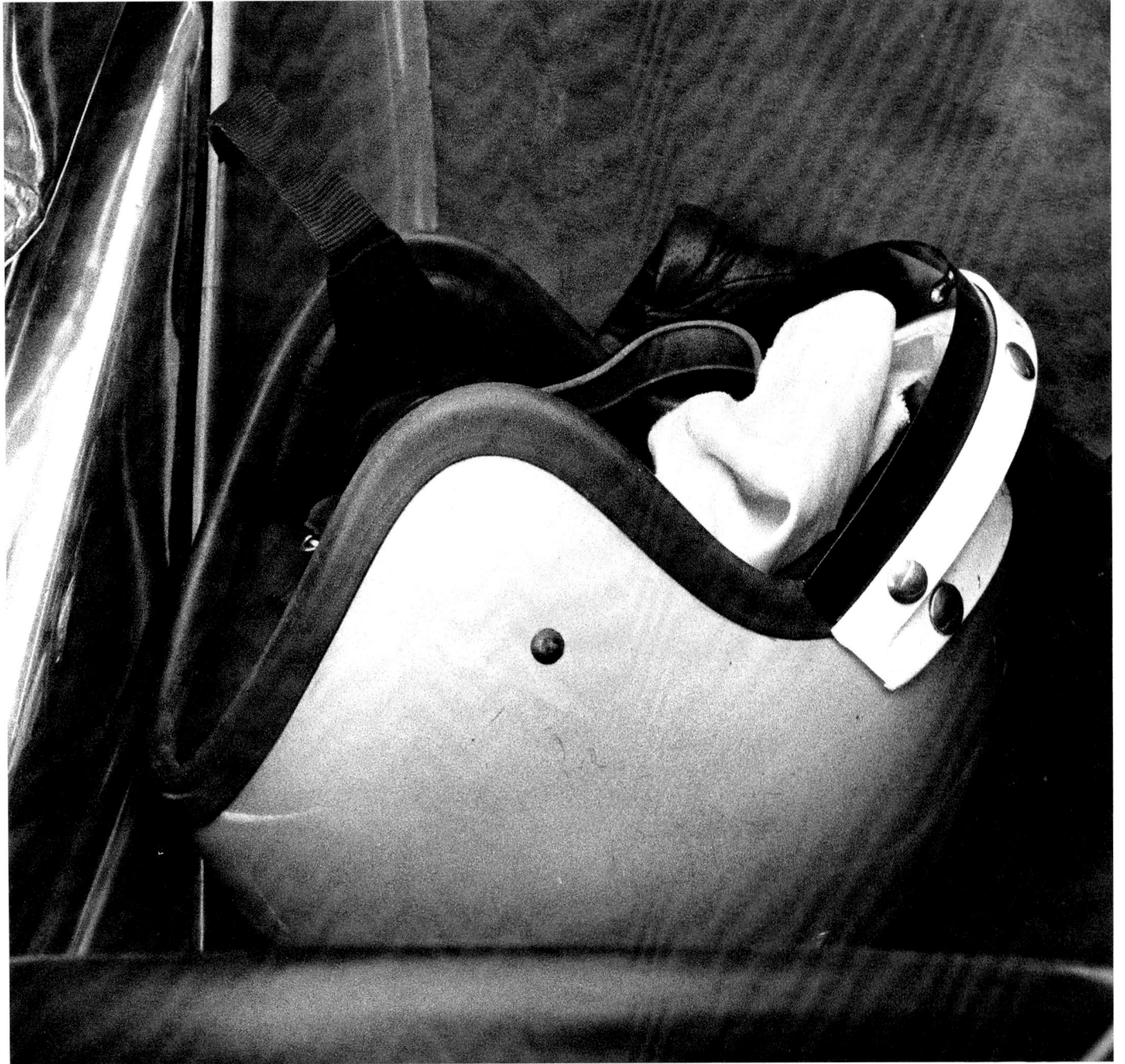

Carroll Shelby, then a partner in All American Racers, Dan Gurney, film actor James Garner, and Ritchie Ginther reflect different moods prior to the start of the 1966 United States Grand Prix.

The usually serious Jochen Rindt enjoys the wit of Chris Amon in 1967.

Jack Brabham and Denis Hulme each won a world title while they were teammates at Repco Brabham during 1966 and 1967.

Graham Hill lights up the tires of his Lotus 49B during the start of the British Grand Prix at Brands Hatch on July 20, 1968. Behind Hill is Lotus teammate Jackie Oliver and Chris Amon in a Ferrari 312. Hill went on to become World Champion that year.

One of the most popular and beautiful Grand Prix cars ever built was Dan Gurney's AAR Eagle-Westlake. This under-financed effort was helped by hundreds of Americans who sent donations to the team and became members of The Eagle Club. Note the huge gathering of supporters as Gurney leaves the garage area of Watkins Glen to practice for the 1967 United States Grand Prix.

Graham Hill and Colin Chapman before the start of the United States Grand Prix in October, 1969.

Colin Chapman with future world champion Mario Andretti. Andretti was making one of his earliest Grand Prix starts at the United States Grand Prix in October, 1969.

John Surtees, on his way to winning the 1964 world championship in his *white and blue* Ferrari. Due to Ferrari politics, the cars were painted white for the North American Grand Prix races, and entered by Luigi Chinetti's North American Racing Team.

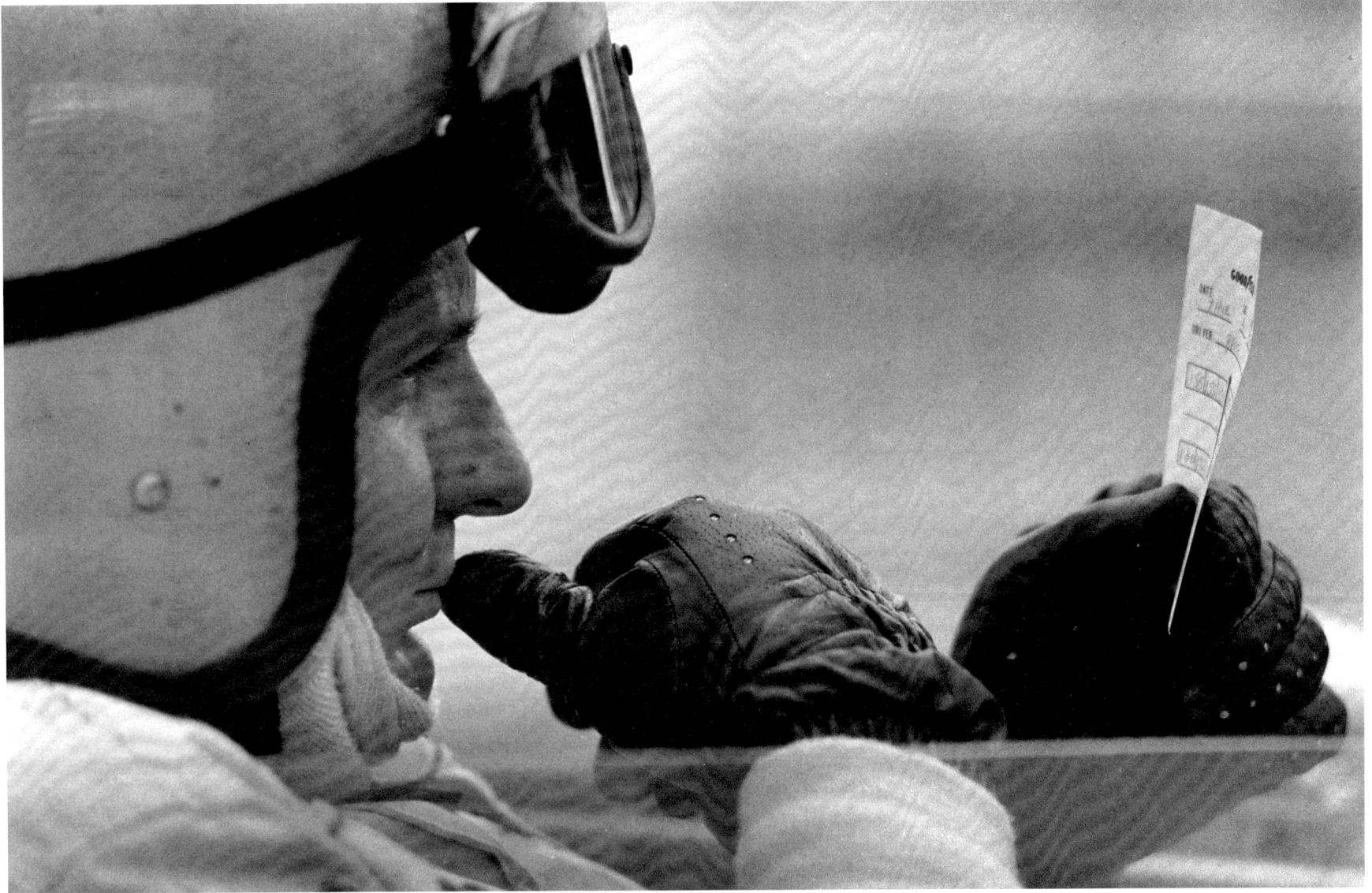

Bruce McLaren, deep in concentration studying his tire report at the Grand Prix of Canada in October, 1969.

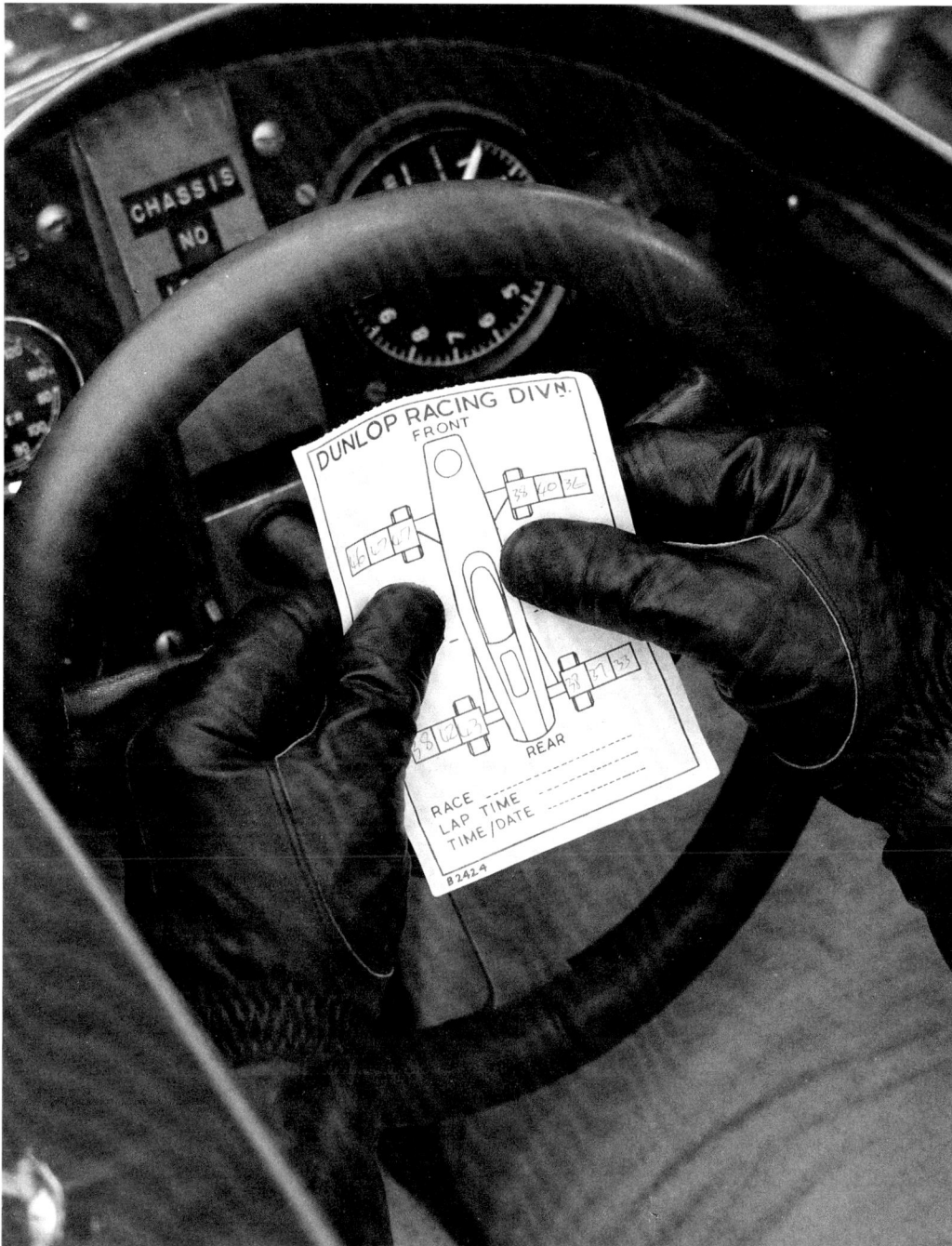

These reports indicate tire wear, temperature, and inflation.
They are used to indicate the best tire combination for the race.

Ken Tyrrell, team manager of the
Matra-Ford Formula 1 effort, was the man
responsible for giving Jackie Stewart the
cars that he needed to showcase his talent.

In 1969, Jackie Stewart won six Grand
Prix races and his first World Championship
driving Ken Tyrrell's Matra-Ford.

Jackie Stewart, World Champion 1969, 1971, 1973.

Emerson Fittipaldi prepares to start the United States Grand Prix in October, 1972.

In 1972, at age 25, Emerson Fittipaldi won 5 Grand Prix races and became the youngest world champion ever.

The beautiful black and gold livery of the John Player Lotus 72D that Fittipaldi drove in 1972 is remembered as one of the most striking color combinations in racing history.

Jochen Rindt was one of Formula 1's most spectacular drivers. Because of his fierce intensity, he was also one of racing's most controversial and charismatic personalities.

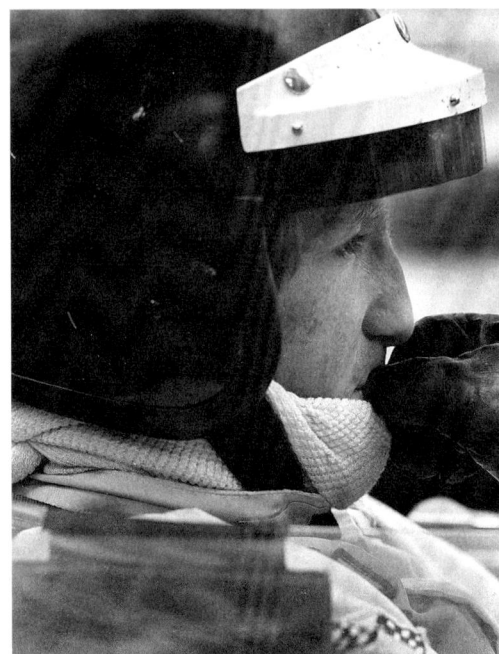

Jochen Rindt, 1970 World Champion. The only driver who never lived to see his championship dream come true. He was killed during practice for the Italian Grand Prix at Monza on September 6, 1970.

After joining the Lotus team in 1969, Rindt drove his Lotus 49B to place fourth in the year's Grand Prix standings.

Jochen Rindt celebrates his first Grand Prix win at the United States Grand Prix on October 5, 1969.

In an era when most of the drivers worked on their own cars, Dan Gurney checks the toe-in of the rear wheels...

Bruce McLaren adjusts the fuel lines and...

Denny Hulme checks the carburetor setup.

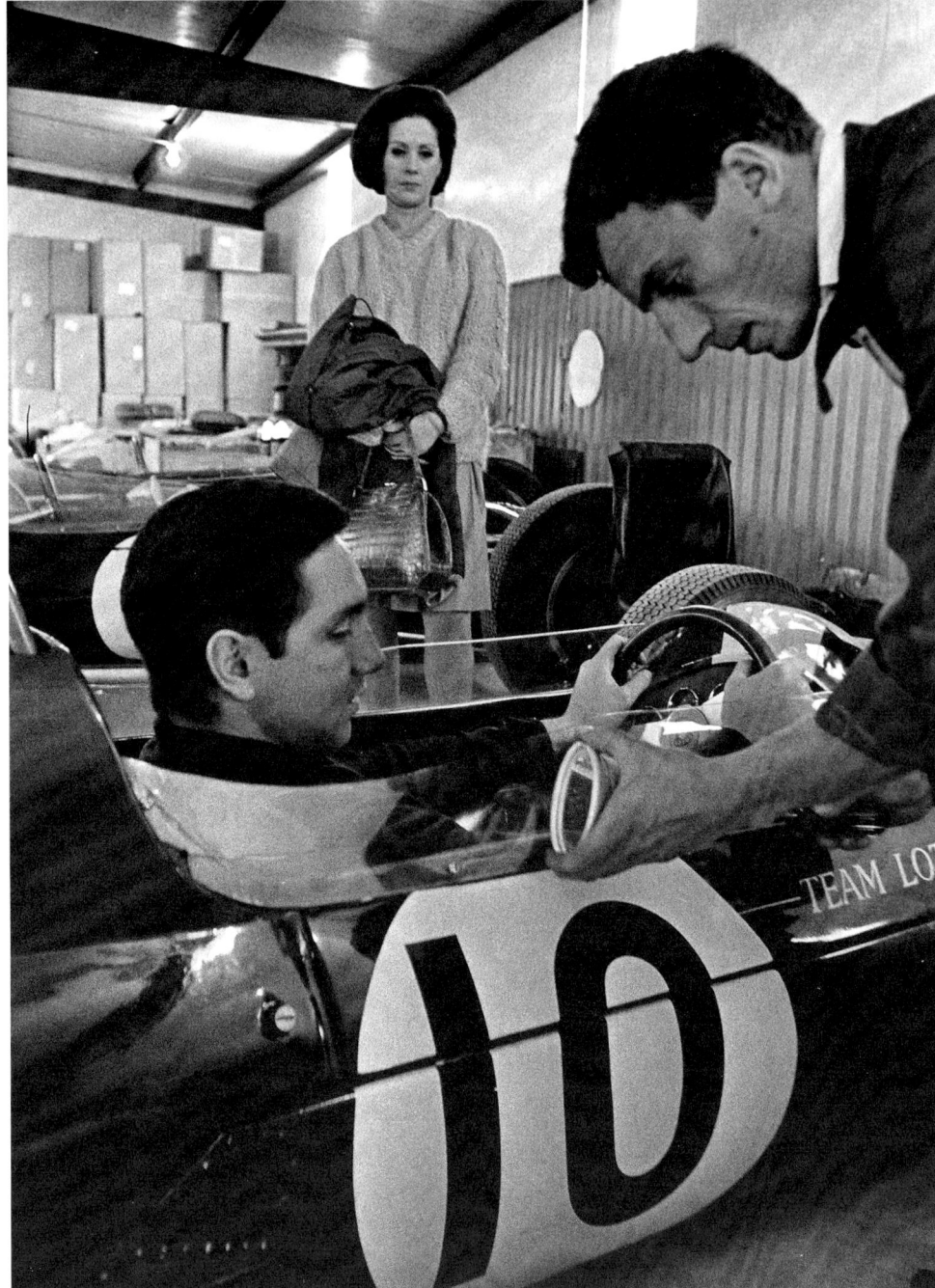

Pedro Rodriguez is fitted to the cockpit of a
Team Lotus 25 as his wife, Angelina, waits in
the background.

Jacky Ickx was a fearless and intelligent driver who never achieved the success in Formula 1 racing that he deserved.

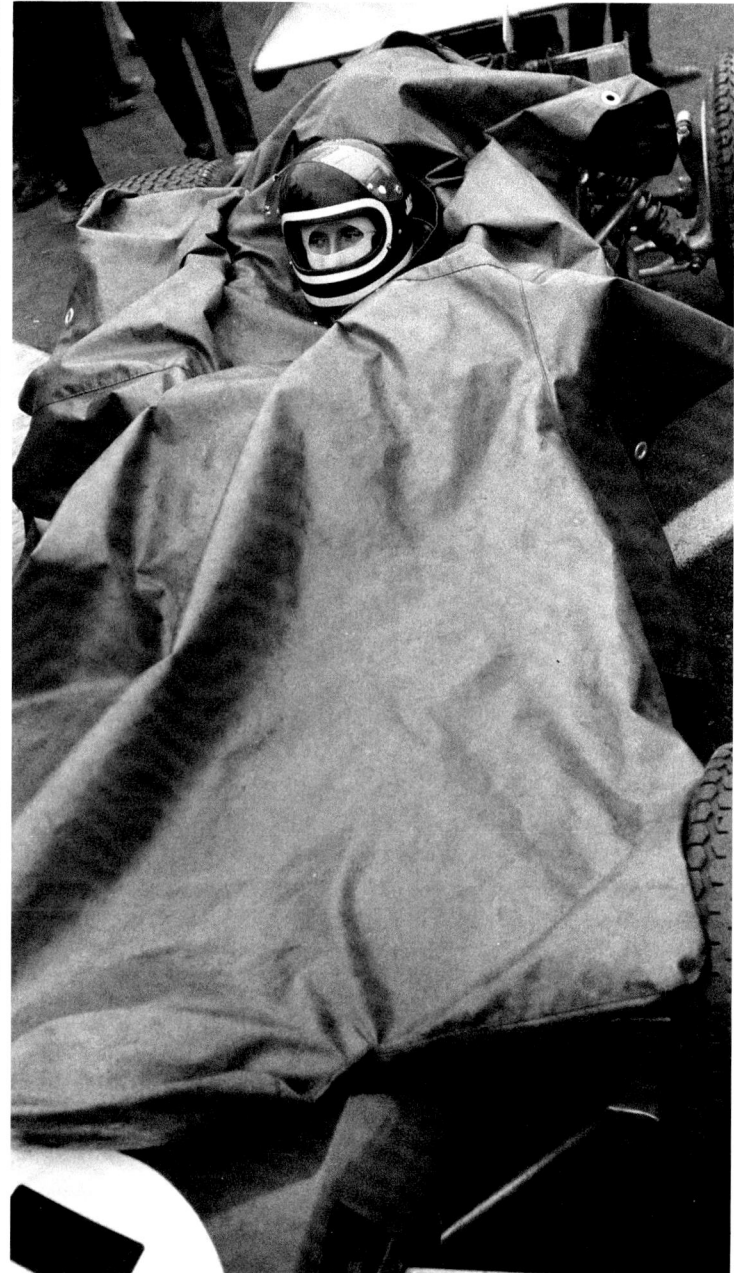

No one has ever been capable of better drives in the rain than Ickx. He was a true "Regenmeister."

John Surtees reaps the spoils of victory at the 1966 Grand Prix of Mexico.

Jim Clark's final victory in the United States came in October, 1967. Celebrating Clark's win are Keith Duckworth of Cosworth and Colin Chapman.

TRANS-AM STOCK CAR

The birth of Trans-Am racing in 1966 gave rise to one of the most exciting series ever conceived. When most people think of Trans-Am racing during that era, they think of the epic battles between Mustang and Camaro, with drivers like Donohue, Titus, Follmer, Jones, and Revson. Few people remember that the first Trans-Am race run at Sebring in March 1966 was indeed won by a two litre Alfa Romeo, driven by a future Formula 1 world champion named Jochen Rindt.

Trans-Am's most epic season was in 1970, when all of the factories took part in the series. It was a year when Camaro, Mustang, Javelin, Dodge, Plymouth and Pontiac battled fender-to-fender with Parnelli Jones winning the championship in his Bud Moore Mustang by one point over Mark Donohue in his Roger Penske Sunoco Javelin.

I remember my first real stock car race because it was on a very cold, wet day at Riverside in March, 1962. The best USAC stock car drivers, Foyt, Jones, Ward, and Ruttman, gathered to race in what was the prelude to the annual NASCAR Grand National 500 Mile event that was to come a year later. A pattern was set that day, when a grand prix star from California named Dan Gurney won the race. Gurney went on to win six of the races in his Woods Brothers prepared Fords and Mercurys between 1963 and his retirement in 1970.

By the time the 1963 race came around, I was thrilled to see the NASCAR stars who never had come west to race. It was the first road race for many of them, but drivers like Roberts, Panch, Petty, Johnson, and Lorenzen caught on pretty fast. It was also the first NASCAR event that was run by many of the USAC drivers. I remember it was run on a very hot day in January and took over six hours to complete.

I regret that I was really never able to see these great stars run at Daytona, although I was able to see some of the short-track races during my visits to the South. The only super-speedway race I was ever able to see was the California 500 at Ontario Motor Speedway.

No two drivers and no two makes of cars better characterized the golden years of Trans-Am racing than Mark Donohue in his Penske Sunoco Camaro and Jerry Titus in the Shelby Mustang. During the 1967 Daytona Trans-Am, Donohue and Titus were fender-to-fender for many laps before Donohue retired with ignition problems and Titus suffered excessive tire wear problems. Daytona was also the first race for the Camaro Z-28.

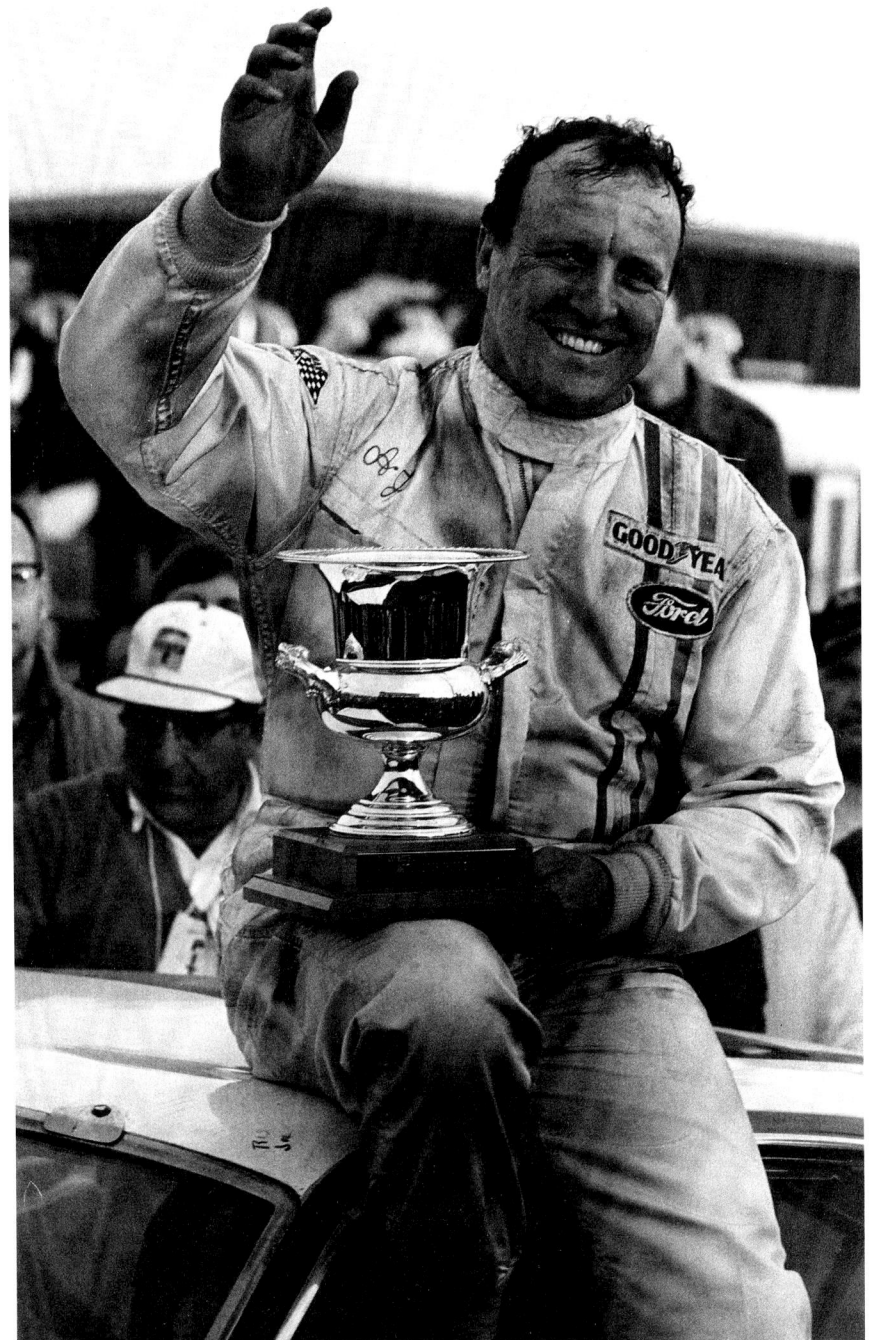

A.J. Foyt celebrates a major NASCAR win at the Riverside 500 in January, 1970. It took Foyt eight attempts and a serious crash before he was able to finally win this event.

In 1969, Richard Petty switched his famous number 43 from Plymouth to Ford. It proved to be a good decision, for he won at Riverside International Raceway, his first time out with the Ford Torino.

Roger Penske receives the winner's garland from Marilyn Fox at the Riverside 250 in May, 1963. Penske, in a rare stock car appearance, nosed out Darel Dieringer for his only stock car win.

Darel Dieringer was one of the first top-level NASCAR drivers to really take to road racing. In November, 1963 he came to the Golden State 400 at Riverside International Raceway as a member of Bill Stroppe's Mercury team and won a very close race with Dave MacDonald, a well known road racer who was driving a Wood Brothers Ford.

Mark Donohue and Roger Penske formed one of the most successful racing teams ever put together. During their years together, they made the "Sunoco Special" a continual winner with top notch management, preparation, and driving skill.

In 1967, the first season for the Penske-Sunoco Camaro Z-28's, the team won three races and finished second in the final Trans-Am standings.

By 1968, the team won ten of the thirteen races held that year including eight in a row. Donohue also won his first of three Trans-Am championships.

The 1969 season brought a repeat championship to Donohue with a record of six wins in twelve races.

Jerry Titus, on his way to victory in the 1967 Sebring Trans-Am race and the series championship. Titus won four of the twelve races in 1967 and emerged as one of the series' most colorful drivers.

Jerry Titus and Carroll Shelby after their big win at the 1967 Sebring Trans-Am. Titus and Shelby proved to be one of the season's most formidable teams.

Jerry Titus and Ronnie Bucknum exchange driving chores during a twilight pit stop at the 1968 Daytona 24 hour race.
The Shelby Mustang finished an amazing fourth overall and first in the Trans-Am class.

Trans-Am racing at its best. Jerry Titus and Parnelli Jones battle for the lead at Daytona in February, 1967.

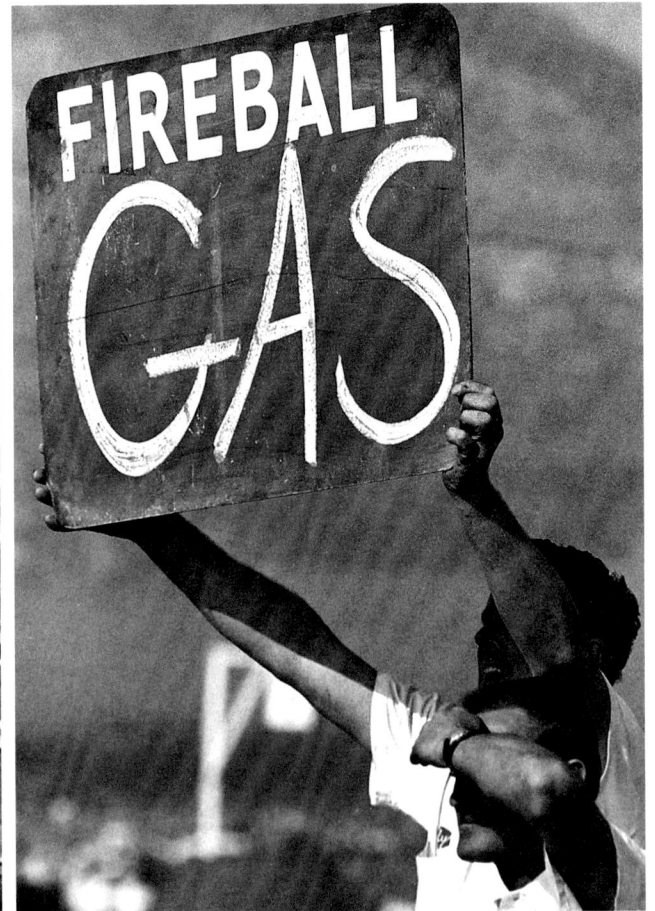

Before the era of radio communications the pit crewmen played an integral part in the communication between the driver and his crew.

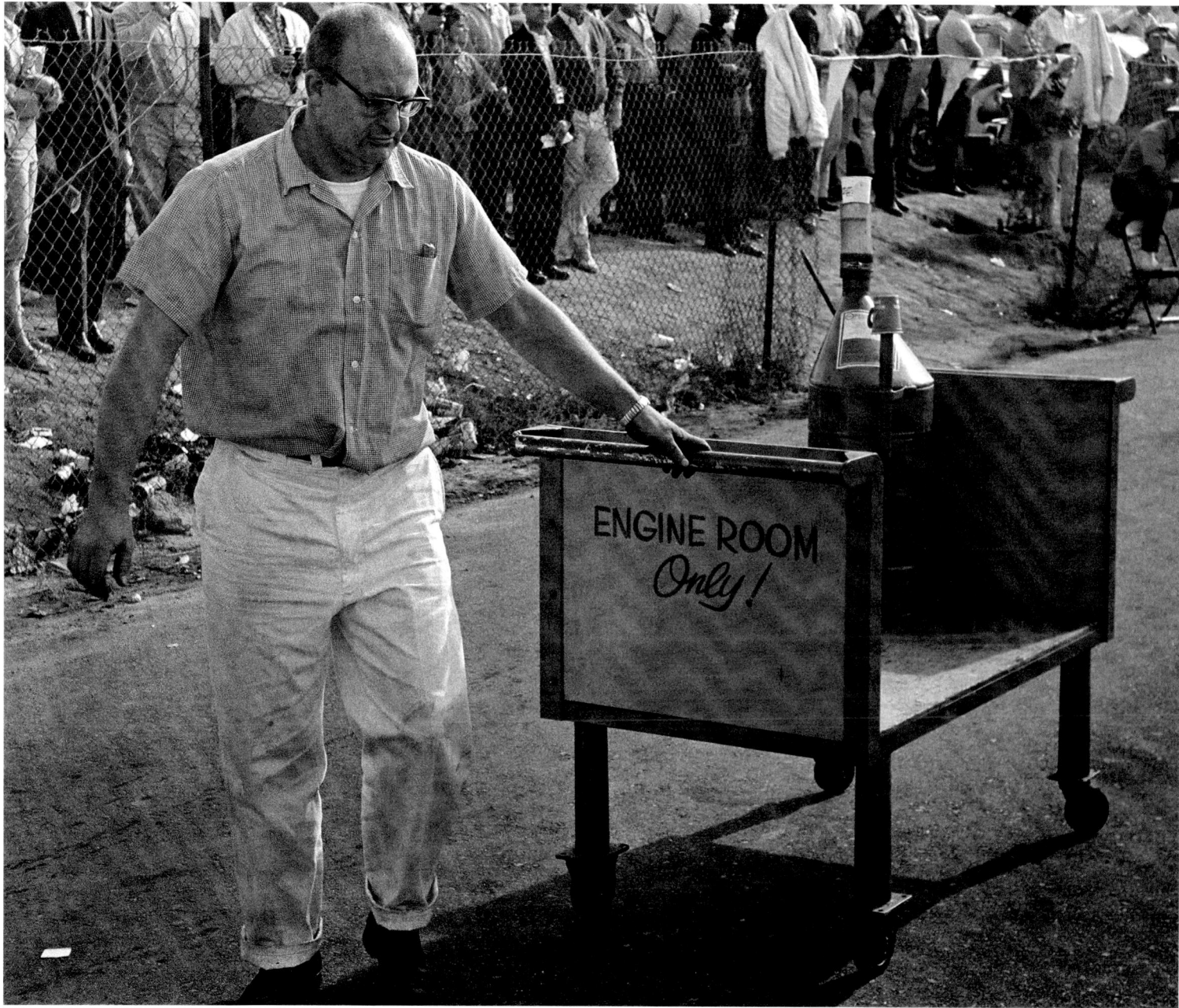

One of stock car racing's most dominant people during this era was John Holman of Holman and Moody. This company was responsible for most of the Ford racing cars run at that time.

"The toughest race I ever drove." Dan Gurney after winning the Green Valley, Texas Trans-Am race in April, 1967.

Dan Gurney (98) nips teammate Parnelli Jones in the closest finish ever in a Trans-Am race, at Green Valley. Gurney remembers the race as "Being so hot in the car, at least 130 degrees, that I had to knock out the side window in order to get all of the air that I could. I was so dehydrated by the end of the race that I could not have made another lap without passing out. It took me three weeks to recover from that experience."

One of the hardest charging teams ever in Trans-Am was the Bud Moore Mustang duo of George Follmer and Parnelli Jones. Mark Donohue said of these two, "When you have Parnelli and Follmer working you over, you have to be careful, they will sacrifice a car and still win." Follmer replied, "We were paid to win and that's what we came to do." Parnelli said, "If you weren't ready, someone would blow your doors off—that wasn't going to happen to me."

Mark Donohue and Peter Revson switched to Javelin for the 1970 season. Under the Penske-Sunoco team leadership, Donohue gave Javelin its first victory at Bridgehampton in June of 1970.

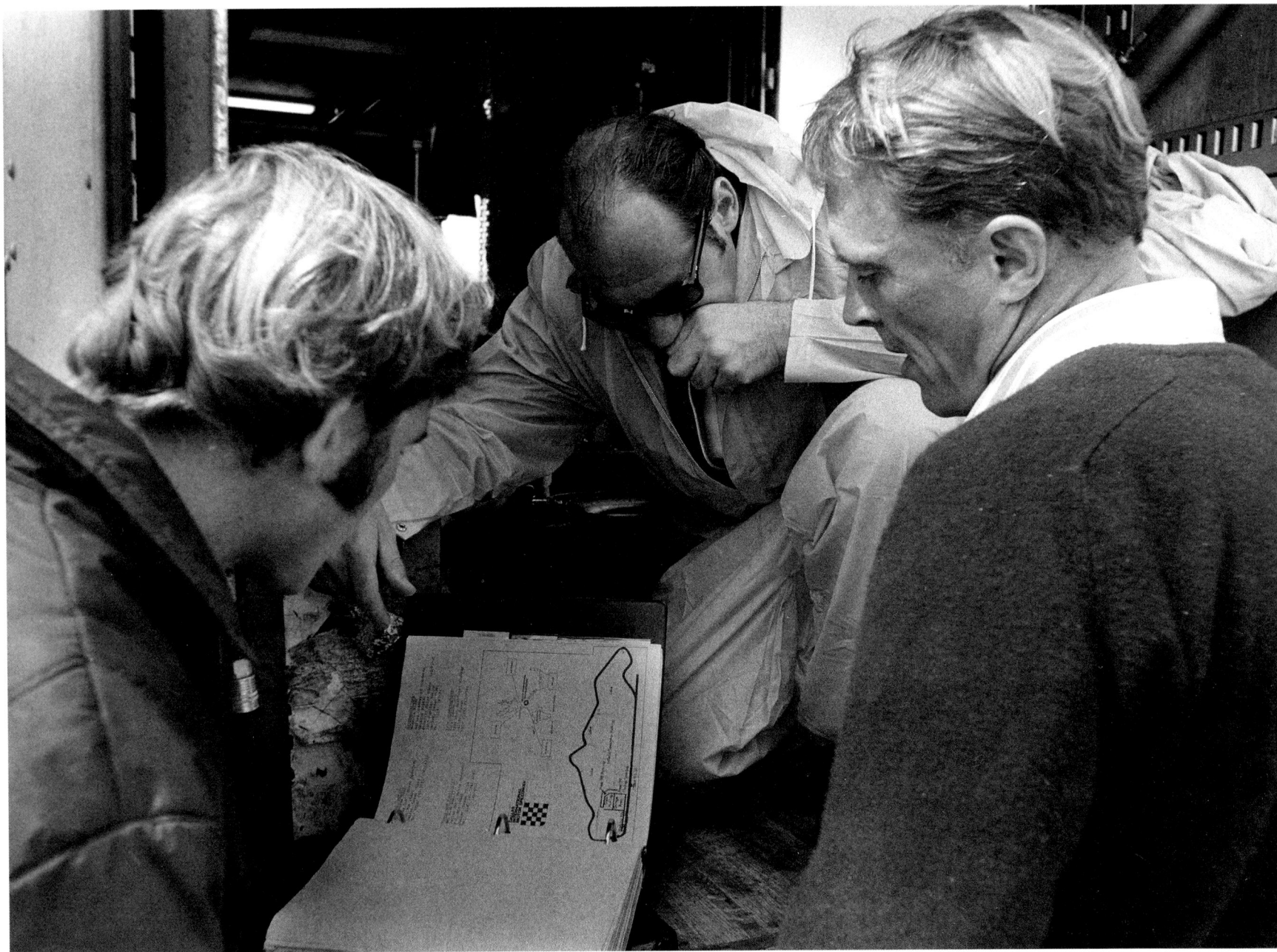

The 1970 Plymouth-Barracuda team of Swede Savage and Dan Gurney review the new track layout at Dallas International Raceway with one of the team mechanics. This race was canceled due to a torrential rainstorm that flooded the track.

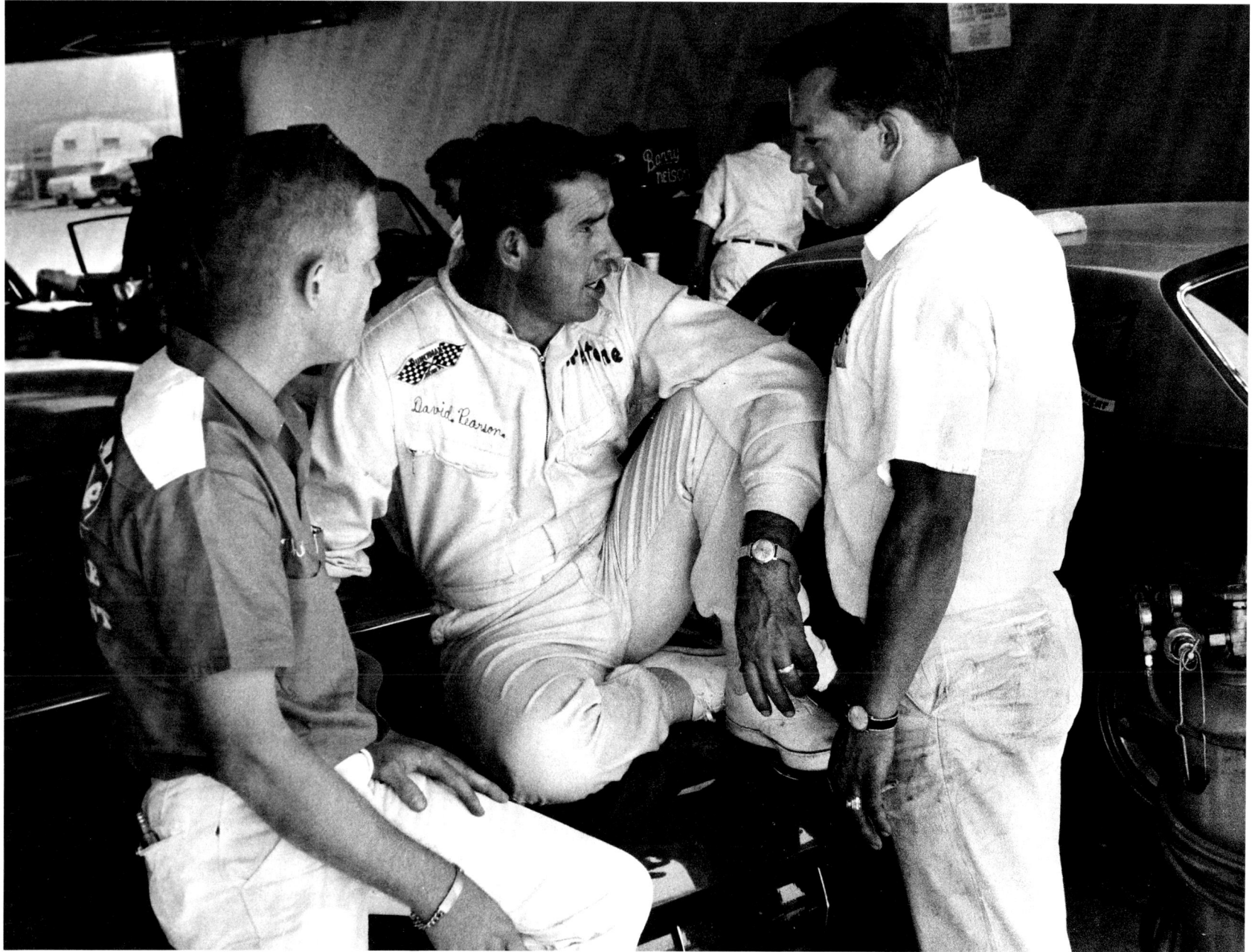

Top NASCAR driver David Pearson made a rare Trans-Am appearance at Riverside International Raceway in October, 1967. Pearson, driving for the Bud Moore Mercury Cougar team won the race that day, his only win in Trans-Am.

Junior Johnson, one of NASCAR's first great drivers of the modern era, races to a second place finish at the Riverside 500 in January, 1965. This was to be Johnson's final season of driving and he would finish the season with 13 wins.

After retiring from driving at the end of the 1965 season,
Junior Johnson became a highly successful team owner.

One of the most successful driver-owner combinations in the history of NASCAR road racing was that of Dan Gurney and Leonard Wood and his famous brothers. This combination won five of the eight races at Riverside International Raceway that they competed in, including four in a row from 1963 to 1966.

Dan Gurney responds to the cheering crowd after winning his fourth consecutive Riverside 500 in January, 1966. Gurney's popularity at Riverside was unlike anything seen elsewhere.

Peter Revson, driving a Boss 302 Mustang for Shelby Racing, crests the top of the esses at Watkins Glen in August, 1969. This was the final year of the famed Shelby racing program.

Many people took Peter Revson to be a playboy racer, but how wrong they were. Revson made his mark in all types of racing, from Indianapolis cars to Formula 1. He became the first American driver to win the Can-Am championship in 1971. Sadly, he was killed in South Africa in early 1974.

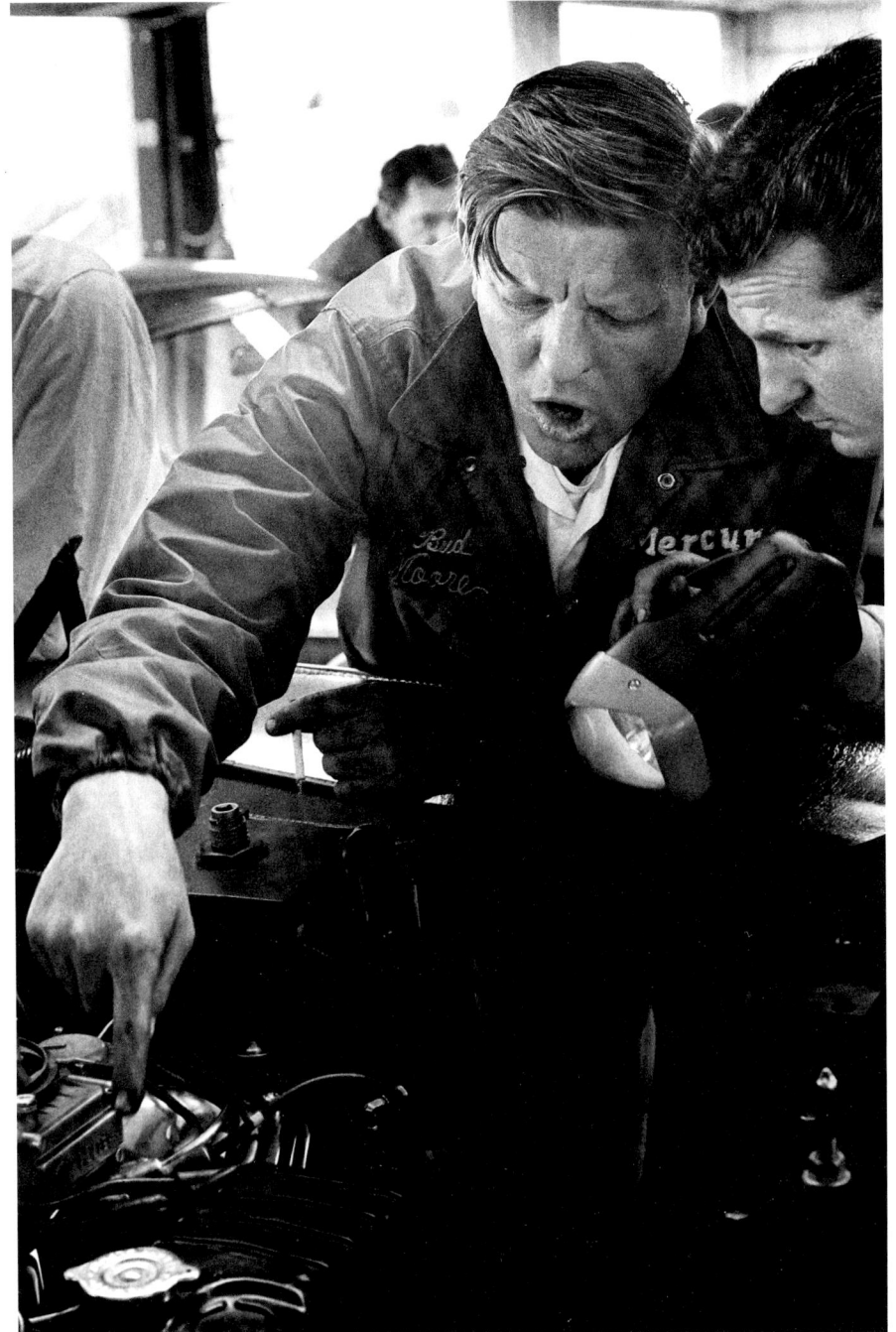

Bud Moore was one of the most successful car owners and mechanics in both Trans-Am and NASCAR.

George Follmer, always known as a hard charger, preparing for the 1969 Watkins Glen Trans-Am.

David Pearson, in his 1970 Holman-Moody Ford Torino, enters Turn 6 at the Riverside 500. Pearson was a top NASCAR driver for many years and always a crowd favorite.

David Pearson — 3 Time NASCAR Grand National Champion.

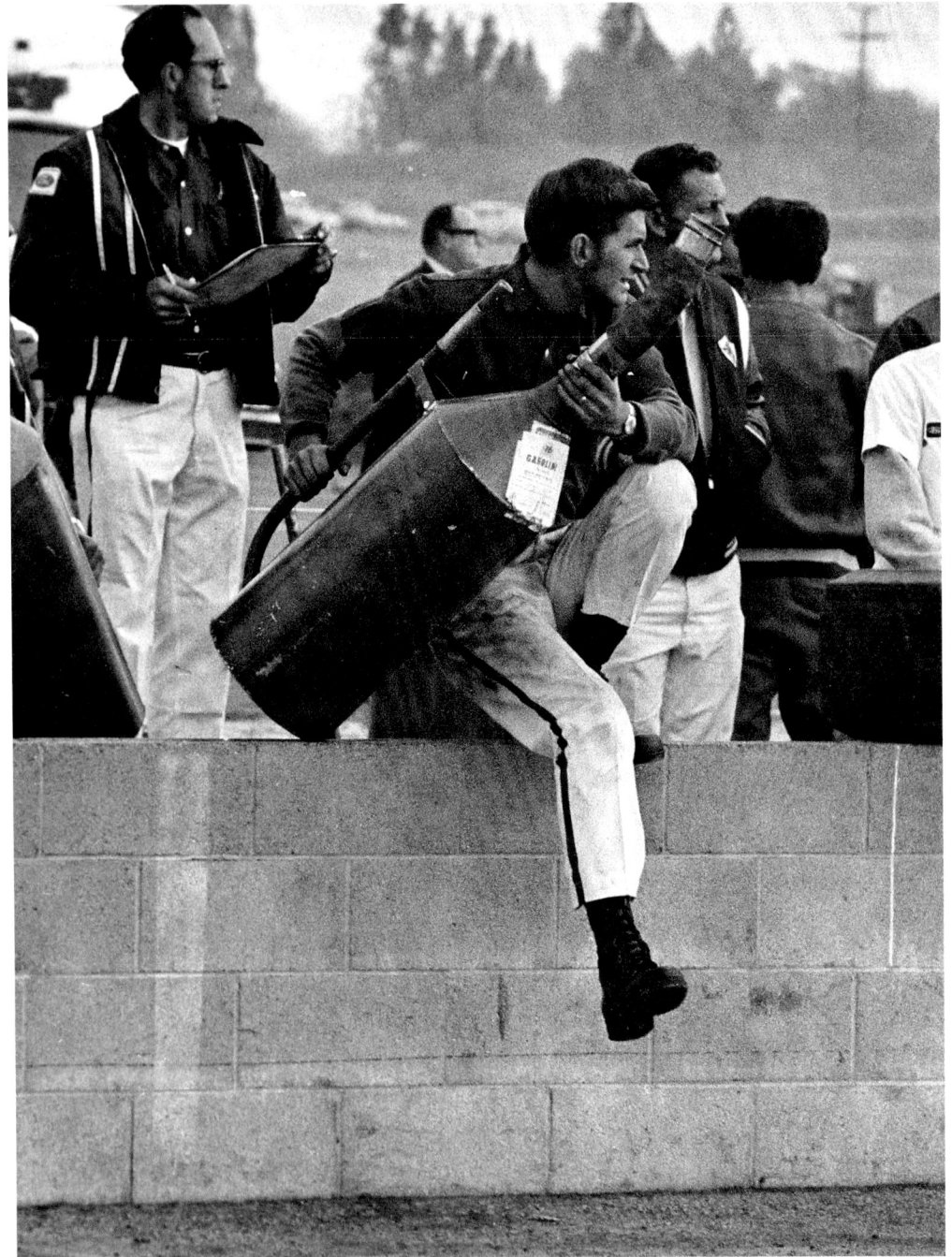

Poised on the pit wall, the fuel man for the Wood Brothers
Mercury team anticipates his driver's momentary pit stop.

As the Holman-Moody crew goes to work, David Pearson tries to check the front end damage from the driver's window.

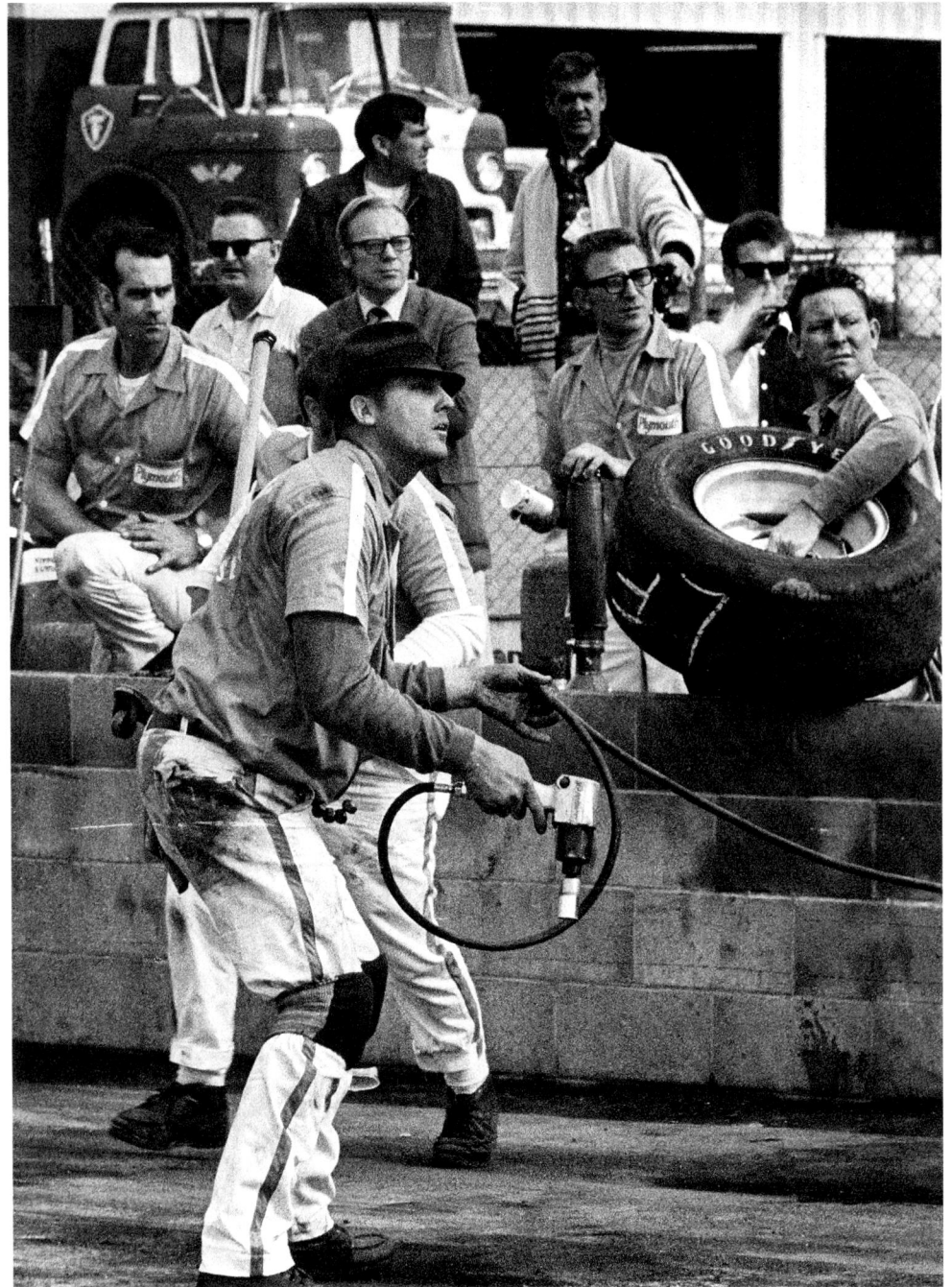

The intensity of this tire changer illustrates the importance of a good pit crew. Numerous races have been lost due to miscommunication between the driver and pit crew. These crews pride themselves on being able to do a fast, efficient job.

This photograph illustrates why the concern for fire safety in the pits is so important. As the fuel man pulls the hose out of the tank, fuel is still flowing from the hose, causing a serious fire hazard.

Swede Savage in his AAR Plymouth Barracuda leads Mark Donohue, Ed Leslie, and Dean Gregson at the Lime Rock Park Trans-Am in May 1970. Gurney and Savage's Barracudas were always fast and well prepared, but suffered from a lack of development.

Swede Savage was an ex-motorcycle racer who became a protégé of Dan Gurney. Under Gurney's wing, Savage became one of the top young American drivers in the early 1970's. After leaving the Gurney team, Savage was tragically killed while leading the 1973 Indianapolis 500.

A.J. Foyt enjoyed stock car racing and like everything else he tried, he excelled at it. Among Foyt's major wins were the Firecracker 400 at Daytona in 1964 and 1965, the Daytona 500 in 1972, and the Motor Trend 500 at Riverside in 1970.

A.J. Foyt on his way to victory in the Motor Trend 500 at Riverside in January, 1970. Foyt is driving Jack Bowsher's Ford Torino.

By 1970, Richard Petty had switched back to Plymouth after one season with Ford. This was the year of the famous Plymouth Superbird and Petty's team won several super-speedway races.

Richard Petty—7 time NASCAR Grand National Champion and one of the most popular drivers in the history of the sport.

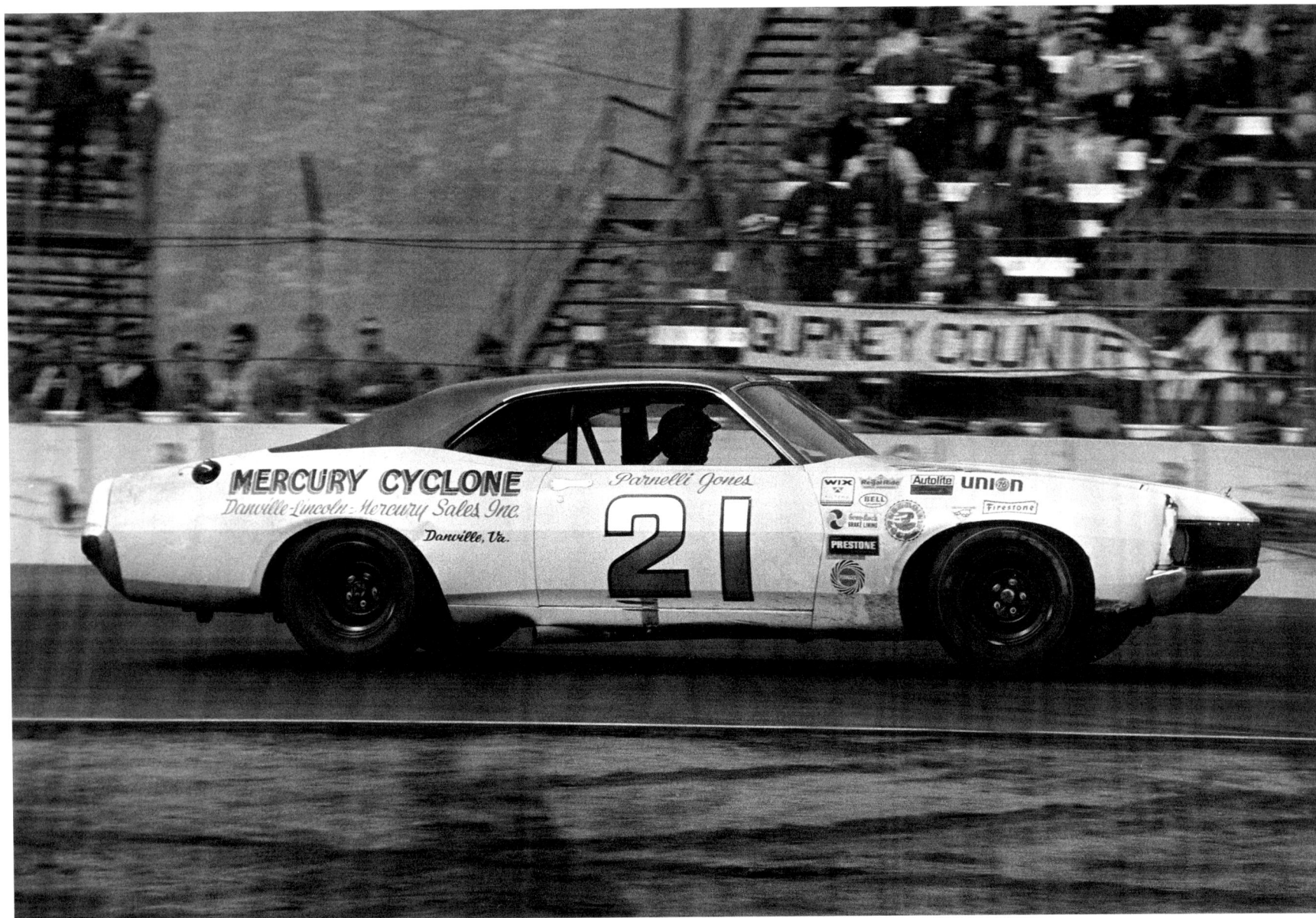

Parnelli Jones, another of the great all around drivers of the era. Parnelli won a number of stock car races, his biggest win at Riverside in 1967. Jones is driving the Wood Brothers Mercury Cyclone at Riverside in January 1970, where he went out of the race with a blown clutch. Note the "Gurney Country" sign in the background.

Parnelli Jones was one of racing's most intimidating drivers. Jones, who began his racing career on small dirt tracks, was always capable of handling whatever type of racing he tried.

Roger McClusky—Two time USAC Stock Car Champion.

Cale Yarborough — Three time NASCAR Grand National Champion.

Lee Roy Yarbrough — Many time winner during his successful stock car racing career. Yarbrough was one of the few NASCAR drivers to attempt Indianapolis cars.

Bobby Allison, NASCAR Winston Cup Champion in 1984, was one of stock car racing's most beloved drivers. Allison was also one of NASCAR's most versatile drivers, having driven Indianapolis cars, Trans-Am cars, and Can-Am cars.

During the 1970 season, Allison drove the Mario Rossi Dodge Daytona. During that season, Allison won two races and finished second in the Grand National championship.

Judy Stropus re-wrote the book on the important job of timing and scoring. She worked for a number of top teams during the late 1960's and 1970's including Bud Moore, Javelin, and Penske Racing.

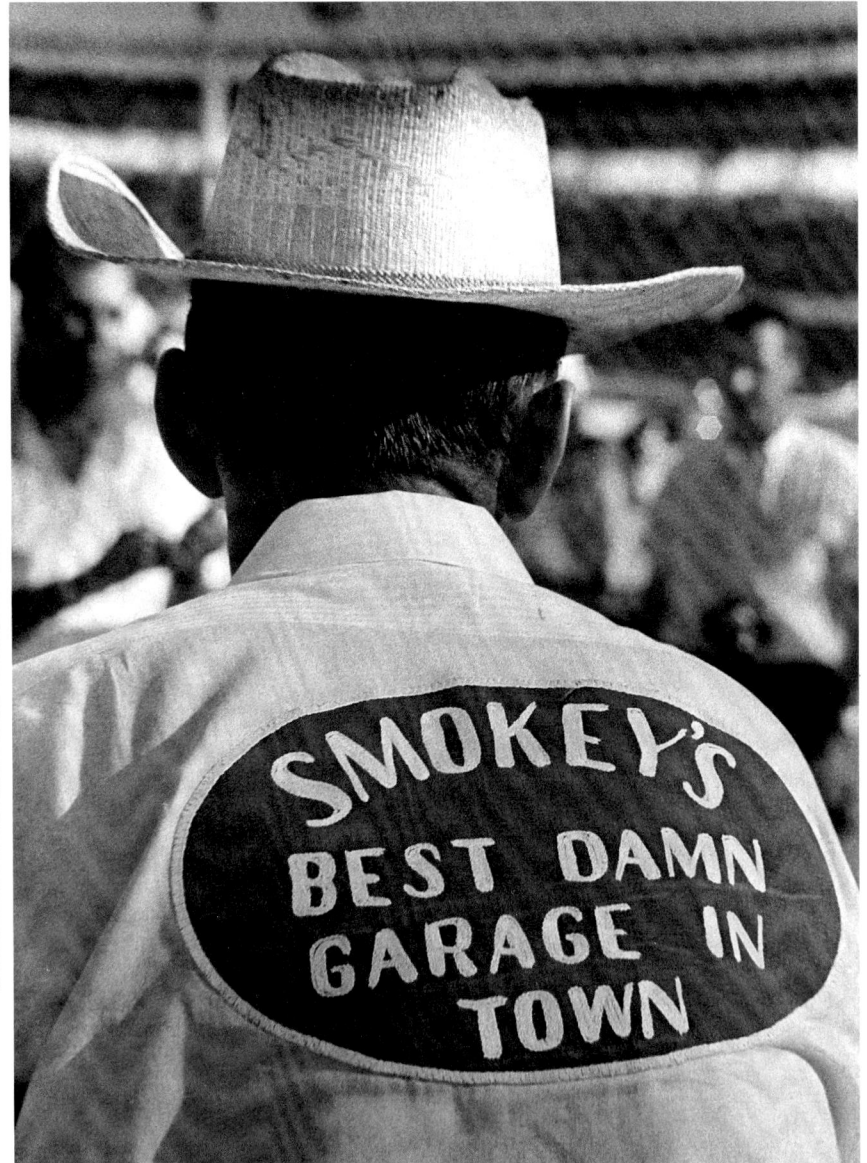

Smokey Yunick was truly a legendary innovator.

During the 1970 Riverside Trans-Am race, Peter Revson and Sam Posey had a slight difference of opinion over who had the proper line through the corner.

Roger Penske, Mark Donohue, and crew discuss gear selection at the Michigan Trans-Am in July 1969.

Jerry Titus helping his crew assemble the fueling rig for the
Watkins Glen Trans-Am, August, 1969.

Richard Petty checking the brake cooling on his Ford prior to the 1969 Riverside 500.

Bud Moore and his crew rushing to complete an engine change
before the start of the St. Jovite Trans-Am in August, 1969.

Parnelli Jones racing in the rain on the banked track at Michigan International Raceway during the July, 1969 Trans-Am event.

The Bud Moore crew in action during a pit stop at Riverside International Raceway in October, 1970.

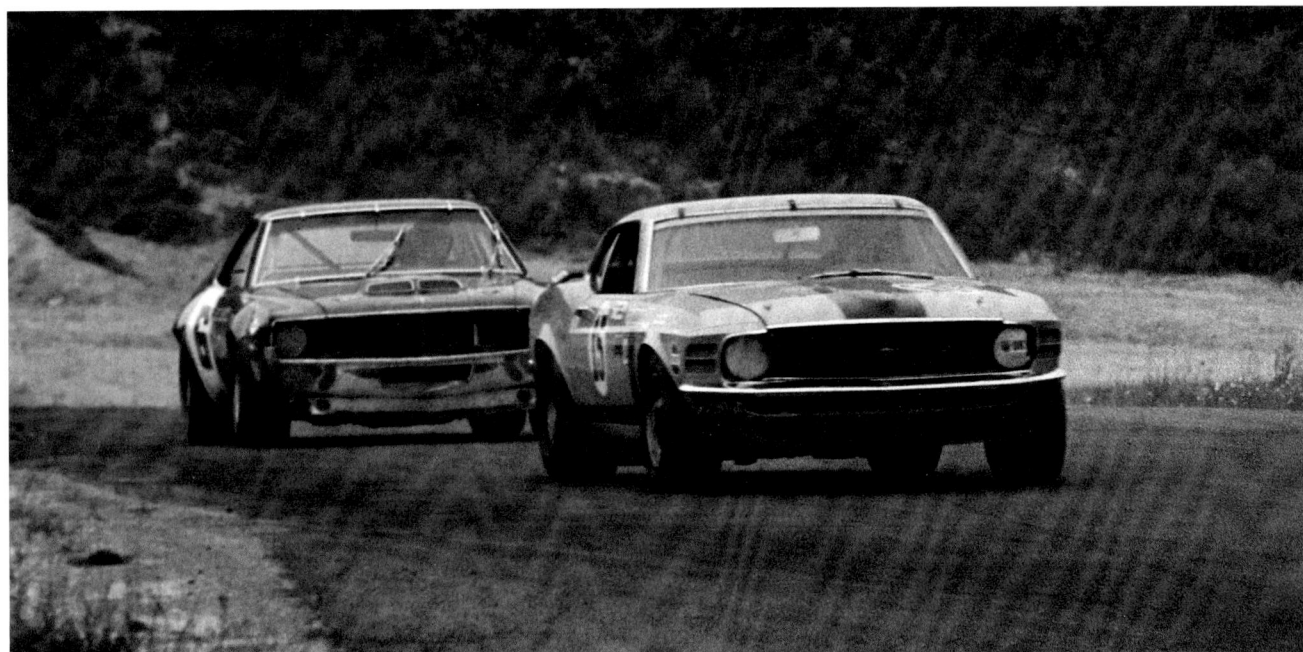

1970 was Trans-Am's greatest year. It was the one year that all of the factories participated. Parnelli Jones driving Bud Moore's Boss 302 Mustang won the year end championship from Mark Donohue's Sunoco Javelin by one point.

Jim Hall and Ed Leslie racing the Chaparral Camaro's in the 1970 Trans-Am season. Hall dropped out in mid-season and Vic Elford took over to give Camaro its only victory at Watkins Glen in August.

Sam Posey driving the factory supported Dodge Challenger during the 1970 season.

Dan Gurney and Swede Savage were the Plymouth Barracuda team for the 1970 season. This was Chrysler's first and last venture into Trans-Am racing.

By 1971 all of the factories, except Javelin, had dropped out of the Trans-Am series. On a rainy day at Lime Rock Park, Mark Donohue's Javelin passes Peter Gregg in Bud Moore's Mustang enroute to the 1971 championship.

One of the highlights of the 1971 season was the appearance of Bob Tullius driving a six year old Pontiac Tempest at Lime Rock. Starting last in a field of 31, Tullius worked his way up to second before problems set in, causing him to finish well off the pace.

Chris Economaki interviewing Buck Baker before the start of the Riverside 500 in January, 1965.

Parnelli Jones and Bud Moore, together with George Follmer formed one of Trans-Am's most potent teams.

Two of racing's top photographers (Bob Tronolone and Bob D'Olivo) are ready to capture the action from a favorite spot at Riverside International Raceway, the outside of turn six.

What do you do when the race loses interest? You play poker in the pits with Sam Hanks, Chuck Daigh, J.C. Agajanian and Rodger Ward.

Fred Lorenzen—Yankee 300—May, 1965.

One of racing's most famous numbers (59) belonged to Peter Gregg and the Brumos Porsche team. Gregg was a consistent winner in the under two litre division of the Trans-Am. As the series changed its format, Gregg became a dominant force winning back to back championships in 1973 and 1974.

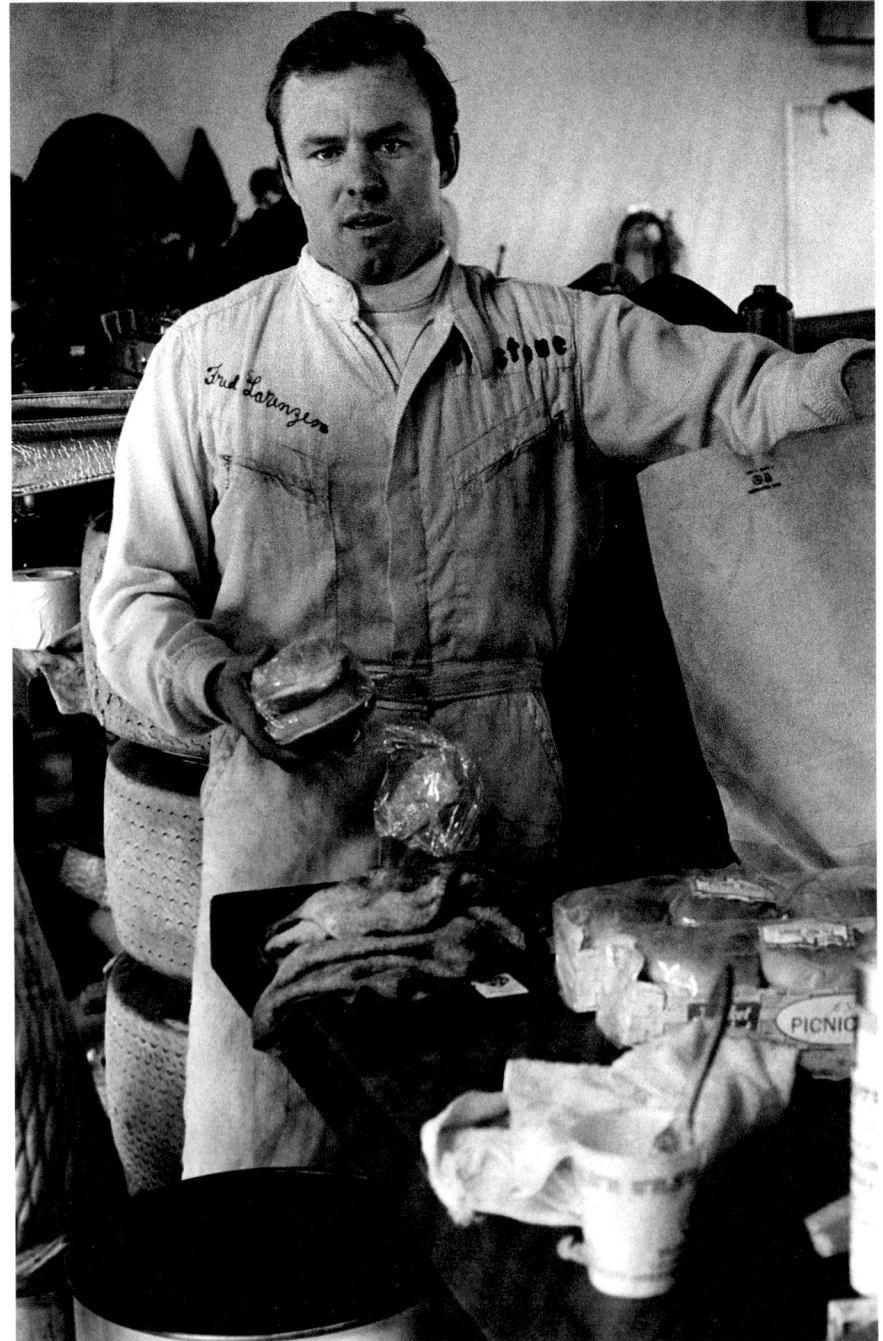

"Fearless Freddie" Lorenzen enjoying a racer's lunch between
practice sessions for the Riverside 500, January, 1967.

Templates used by NASCAR officials to make sure that the cars complied with the proper body configurations.

No one could accuse Holman-Moody of not being prepared when they went racing.

Dick Hutcherson learning the meaning of the long walk back
to the pits after a mishap at the far end of the track.

Glen "Fireball" Roberts was NASCAR's first major super-speedway star. He also ventured into sports cars, driving at Daytona, Sebring, and LeMans. Roberts was killed in a fiery crash at the Charlotte World 600 on May 24, 1964.

A.J. Foyt (21) and Richard Petty (43) lead the first corner charge during the opening laps of the Miller 500 at Ontario Motor Speedway in March, 1972. Foyt was the winner.

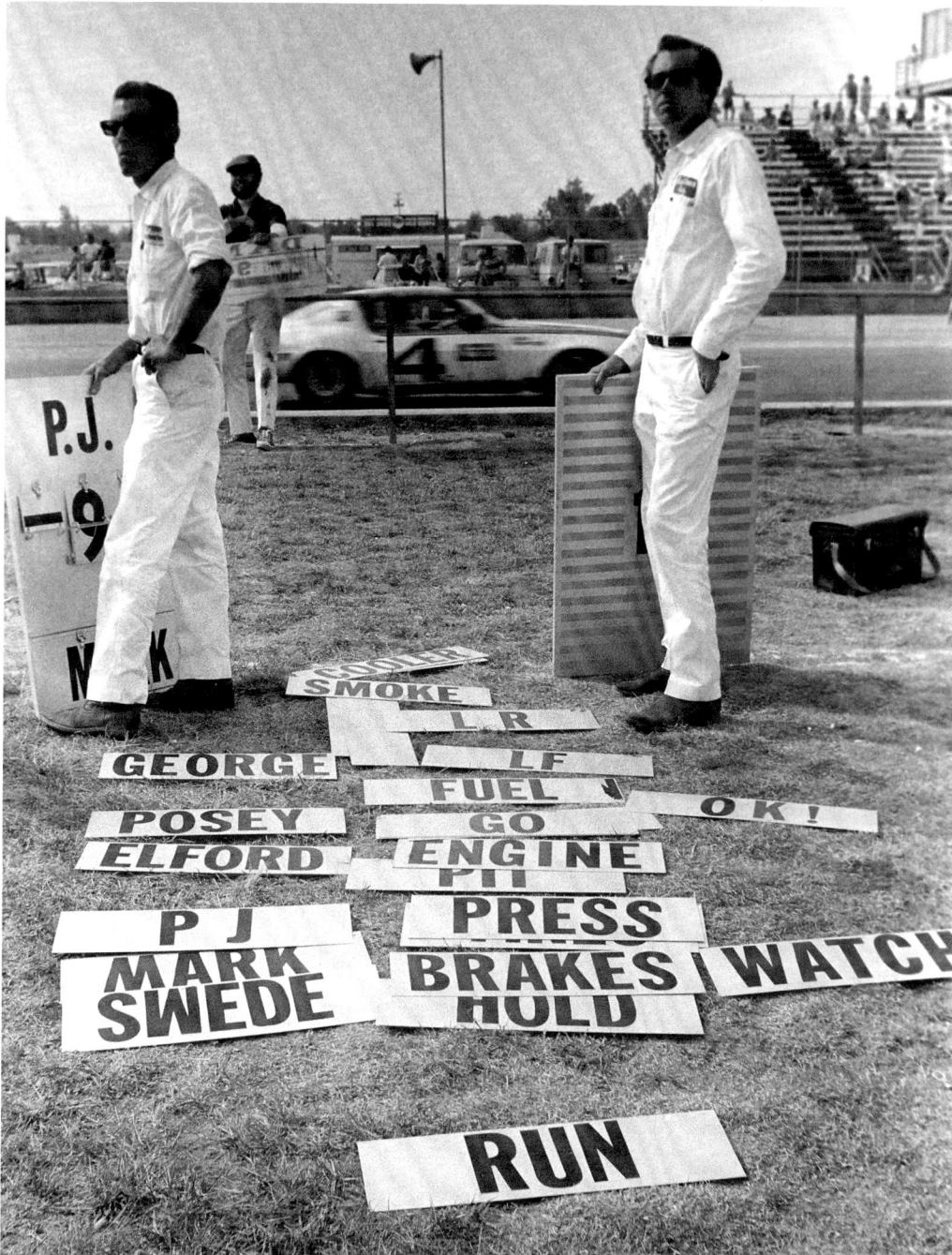

Bud Moore's signal crew waits intently for Follmer and Jones
to appear during the closing laps of the Riverside Trans-Am
race in October, 1970.

Denis Hulme, Can-Am Champion, 1968 and 1970.

SPORTS RACERS

I first became a fan of sports car racing while I was in high school. We attended club events since the advent of professional racing was still several years away. This was a very special time in California club racing — since drivers like Shelby, Gregory, Ginther, Hill, Gurney and so many others who were to make their mark in the years to come, were still racing at the local level.

My first professional sports car race was *The Los Angeles Times Grand Prix for Sports Cars* in October, 1958. After that event, I was hooked. In the years following, sports car racing entered its golden era.

Between 1958 and 1974, I was fortunate enough to have seen all of the great cars and drivers. Who can forget the classic duels between Ford, Ferrari, Chaparral, and Porsche in endurance racing, or the mighty Can-Am cars, the fastest and most powerful sports-racing cars ever built. It was a time when all of the great drivers from Formula 1, Championship Car racing, and even Stock Cars crossed over the line to drive sports cars. The names are legendary: Clark, Hill, Hall, Gurney, Surtees, Stewart, Foyt, Jones, and the list goes on. The fantastic machinery ranged from Reventlow's beautiful Scarab to the super-fast Porsche 917/30 and the Shadow DN4. This was also the beginning and the end of many legendary racing series including: the World Championship for Sports Prototype and GT Cars, the West Coast Pro Series, USRRC, British Group 7 Series, the Interserie, and the ultimate show, The Canadian-American Challenge Cup.

It was all different then. Professionalism was there, but today's overpowering commercialism had not yet affected the sport. Everyone worked together for the betterment of racing. I remember at the Michigan Can-Am in 1969, when mechanics from McLaren, Chaparral, and Lola helped an independent entry with a last-minute engine change so that the car could make the starting grid. I'm not sure that attitude prevails today. When I look back, I realize that sports cars were where my roots were.

This was a time when drivers took a hands-on interest in the preparation of their cars. Jim Clark—Lotus 30—Riverside October, 1964...

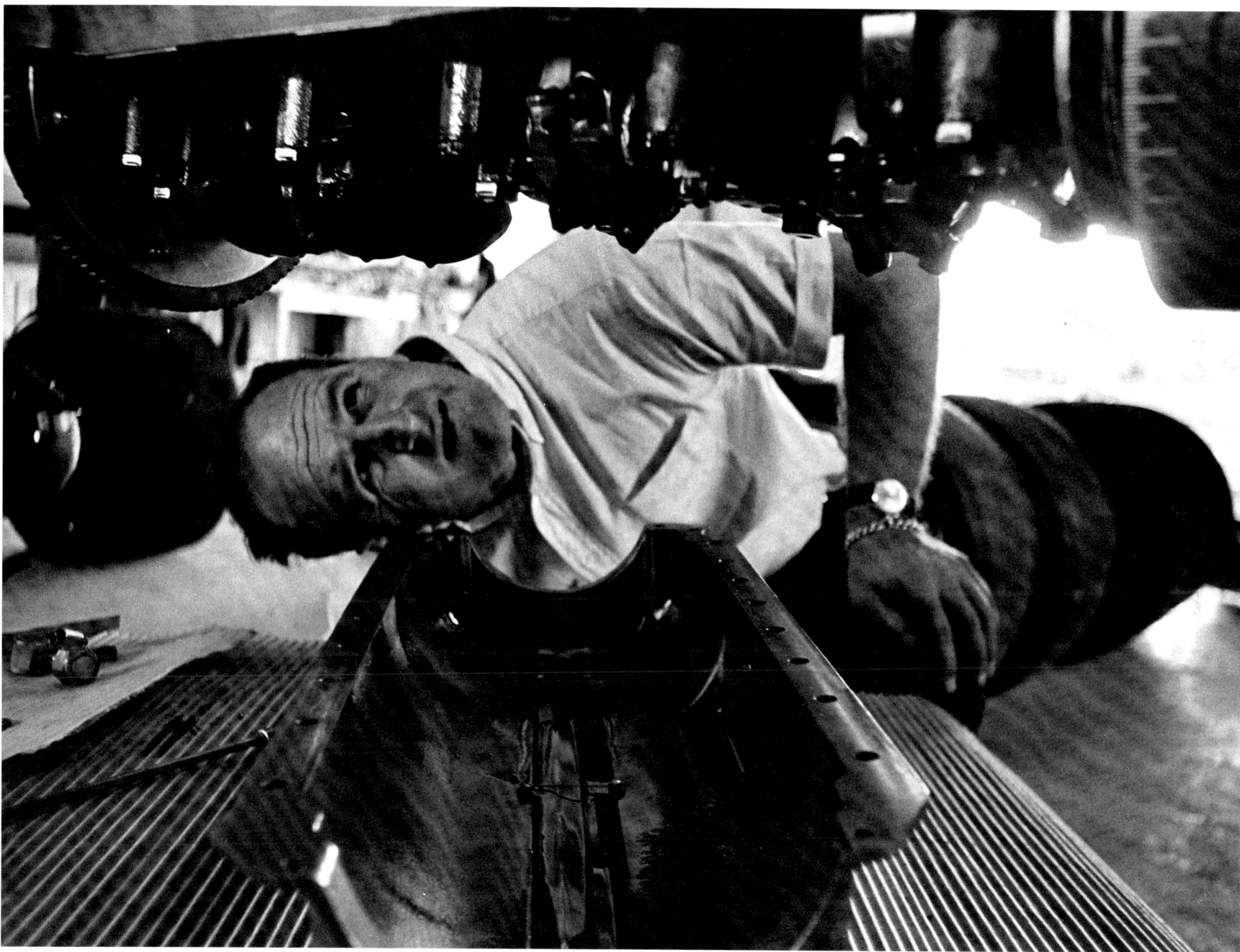

Denis Hulme—McLaren M8A—Road America, September, 1968...

153

Bruce McLaren – McLaren M1A – Laguna Seca – October, 1964...

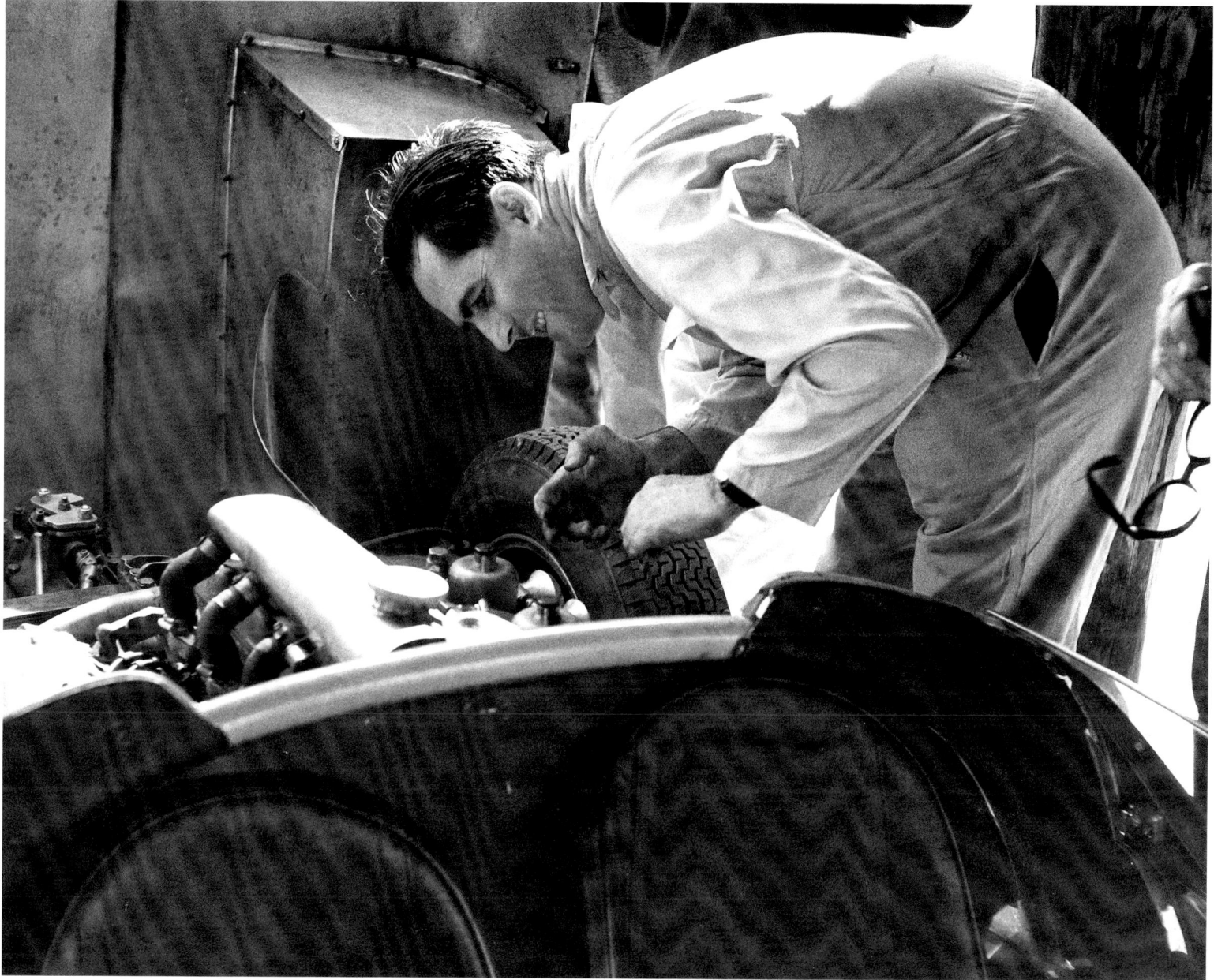

Jack Brabham — Cooper Monaco — Nassau — December, 1959.

Jim Clark's reply to the "Gurney For President" campaign being waged in late 1964.

The Shelby American hanger at Sebring in March 1966. By this time, the Shelby effort was totally committed to the Ford endurance program.

The Chaparral crew burns the midnight oil at Sebring, March 1965. the work paid off as the Chaparral team won the 12 hour race.

Sebring, March, 1962 was the first time that the Chaparral team entered an endurance race. Although the two car effort ran into a number of problems, one car managed to finish sixth overall.

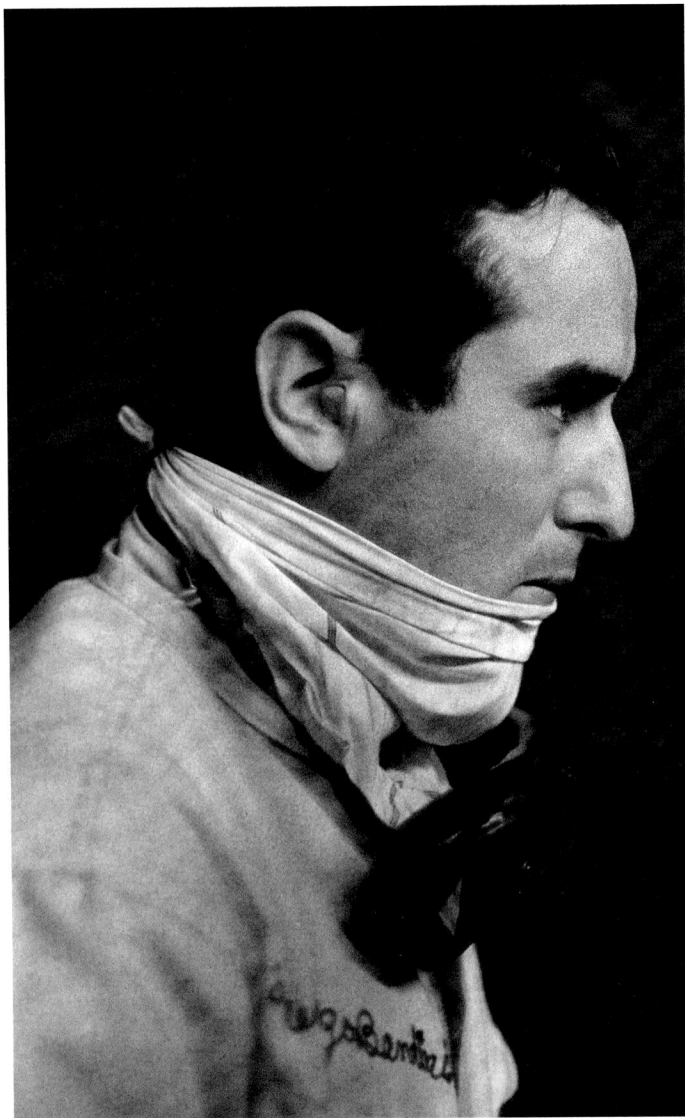

Lorenzo Bandini — Ferrari 330P4 — Daytona 24 Hour —
February, 1967.

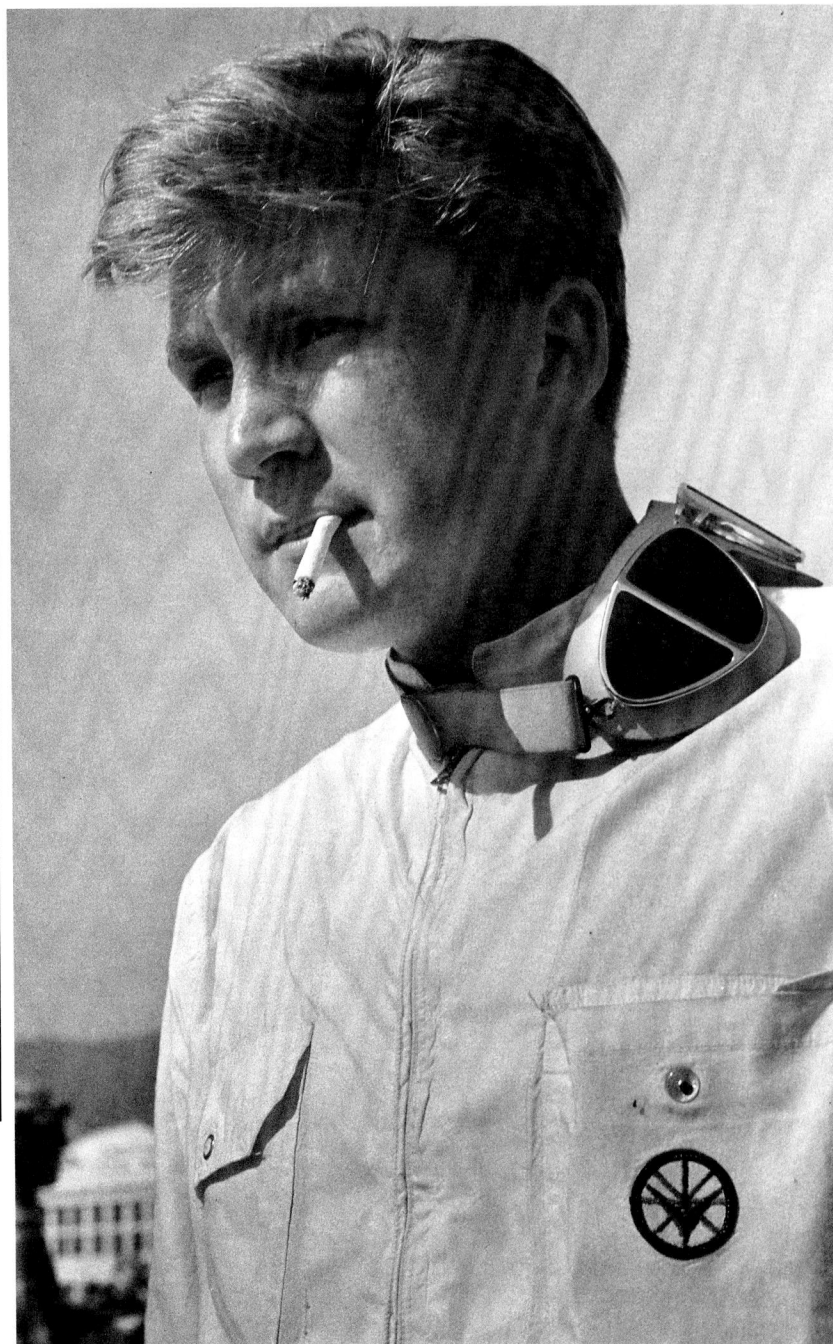

Lance Reventlow — Scarab — Riverside — October, 1958.

Ludovico Scarfiotti—Ferrari 275P—Sebring—March, 1964.

Joakim Bonnier—Porsche Spyder 8 cylinder—Mosport—
September, 1962.

Bruce McLaren celebrates his win at the most prestigious race of the Can-Am season, The Los Angeles Times Grand Prix for Sports Cars at Riverside in October, 1968. Tyler Alexander, McLaren's mechanic, holds the trophy.

Bruce McLaren takes Tyler Alexander for a victory lap after winning the Player's 200 at Mosport Park in Canada. This June 1964 win was the first major success for the fledgling McLaren team. The car driven here by McLaren was the famous ex-Penske Zerex Special often referred to as "The Jolly Green Giant."

Derek Bell was one of endurance racing's greatest drivers, winning LeMans
five times, Daytona three times and the World Championship twice. Bell's
first big break came in 1971 when he was signed to race the Gulf Porsche
917K for John Wyer and he responded with several wins.

Derek Bell at the wheel of the Gulf Mirage during the Watkins Glen 6 Hour race in July, 1972.

Parnelli Jones was one of the many USAC drivers who became successful in sports cars. In his first major sports car race, Jones won the Times Grand Prix in October 1964, driving a Shelby American King Cobra.

During the 1966 Can-Am season, Jones drove a Lola T70 for John Mecom with some success. After 1966, except for a brief appearance in 1967, Jones unfortunately vanished from the Can-Am scene.

Innes Ireland, driving the Rosebud Racing Team Ferrari powered Lotus 19 at Laguna Seca in October, 1964, was one of the most popular of the European drivers to come to America during the Fall Pro Series.

The always dapper Innes Ireland was once voted one of the ten best dressed men in the world.

Augie Pabst, in spite of his reputation as one of the great pranksters in American racing, was a fine driver who won many races in his long career.

Pabst was best known for his many victories in the Meister Brauser Scarab. At Continental Divide Raceway, Pabst gave the front engined Scarab its final victory in August, 1963. The Scarab was one of the most successful sports cars ever, winning many races over a six year period.

Ritchie Ginther was one of the group of California drivers who went to Europe in the early 1960's and made an impact on international racing. Ginther became known as one of the world's best test and development drivers.

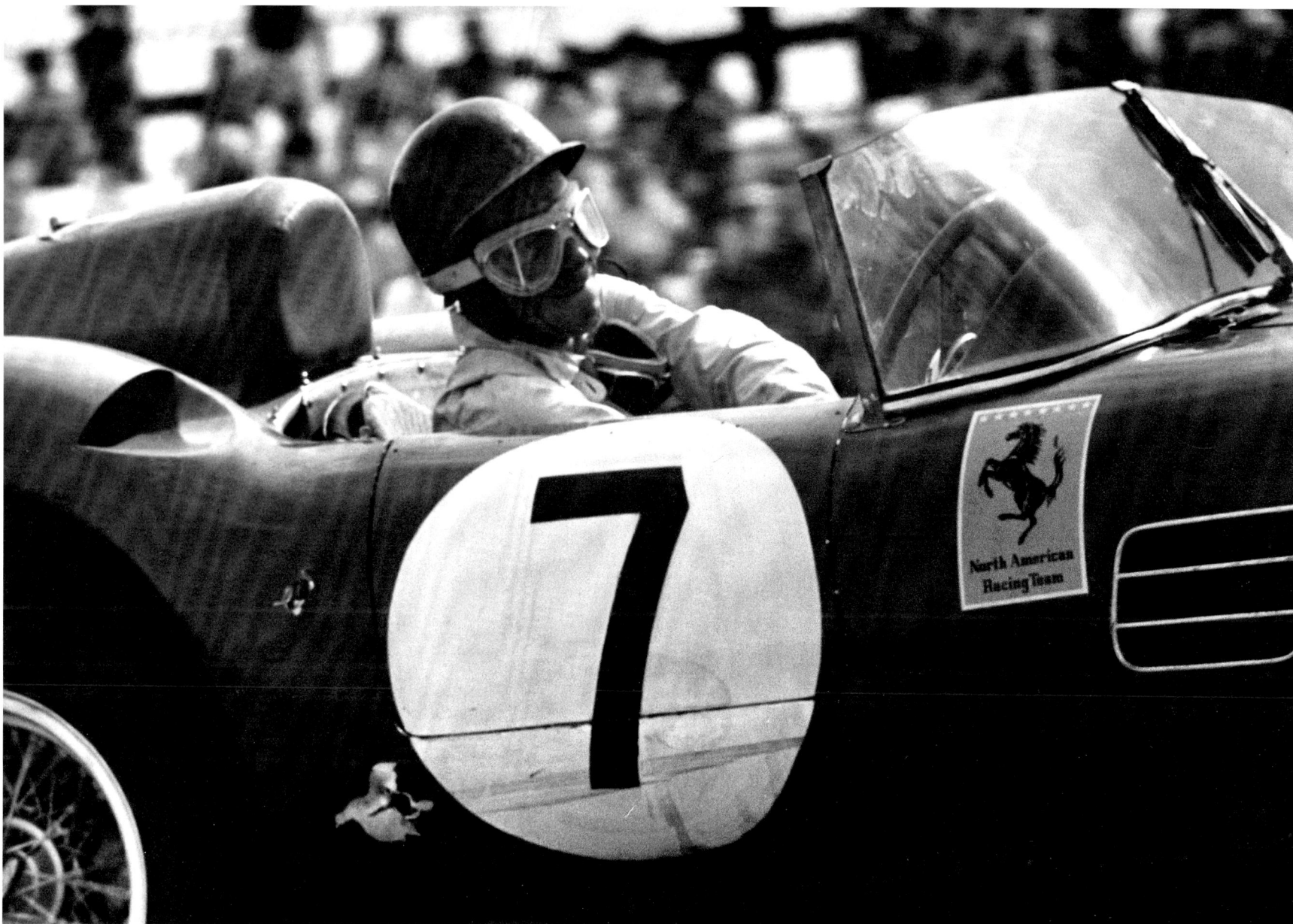

An intense Ritchie Ginther at Sebring in March, 1960.

Mark Donohue and the famous "Sunoco Special" Lola T70 at Las Vegas Can-Am in November, 1967. Donohue had this race won, but ran out of fuel on the last lap and finished second.

Donohue celebrates his win at the Bridgehampton Can-Am in September 1968. Donohue was the only American driver to win a Can-Am race during the 1968 season. He finished third in the overall Can-Am standings behind Denis Hulme and Bruce McLaren.

Pedro Rodriguez was the older of the hard driving Rodriguez brothers. Pedro had a successful career in Formula 1, but it was with John Wyer's Gulf team that he really shined. Rodriguez drove the Gulf Ford GT40's and Porsche 917's to numerous victories before being killed in a 1971 Interserie race in Germany.

Ricardo Rodriguez, the youngest of the Rodriguez brothers, drove with the incredible bravado of a matador during his brief but spectacular racing career. From age 15, when he first appeared on the international scene until he was killed at age 20 during the Mexican Grand Prix in November, 1962, Rodriguez added a colorful Mexican flavor to the sport.

Huschke von Hanstein was the Porsche team manager during the glory years, and he brought Porsche from contender in the under two litre class to dominant overall winner in many of the great races of the world.

The Porsche 197K was one of the greatest sports cars ever built. It was virtually unbeatable during the 1970 and 1971 world sports car championship.

The Porsche 907 was the first Porsche to win a 24 hour race. This occurred at Daytona in February, 1968.

Ken Miles was one of the finest Porsche drivers in America when he signed on with the Shelby Cobra effort in February, 1963. The contributions that Miles made to the Cobra successes were so numerous that it is difficult to list them all, however, the testing and development that he did improved the breed considerably.

He was known as "The Hawk" and numerous other names, but Ken Miles proved that he was one of the finest drivers of the era. With the Shelby Ford GT 40 and Ford Mk.II programs, Miles won at Daytona in 1965 and 1966, Sebring in 1966, and almost at LeMans in 1966. Miles was killed during a Ford J Car test at Riverside in August, 1966.

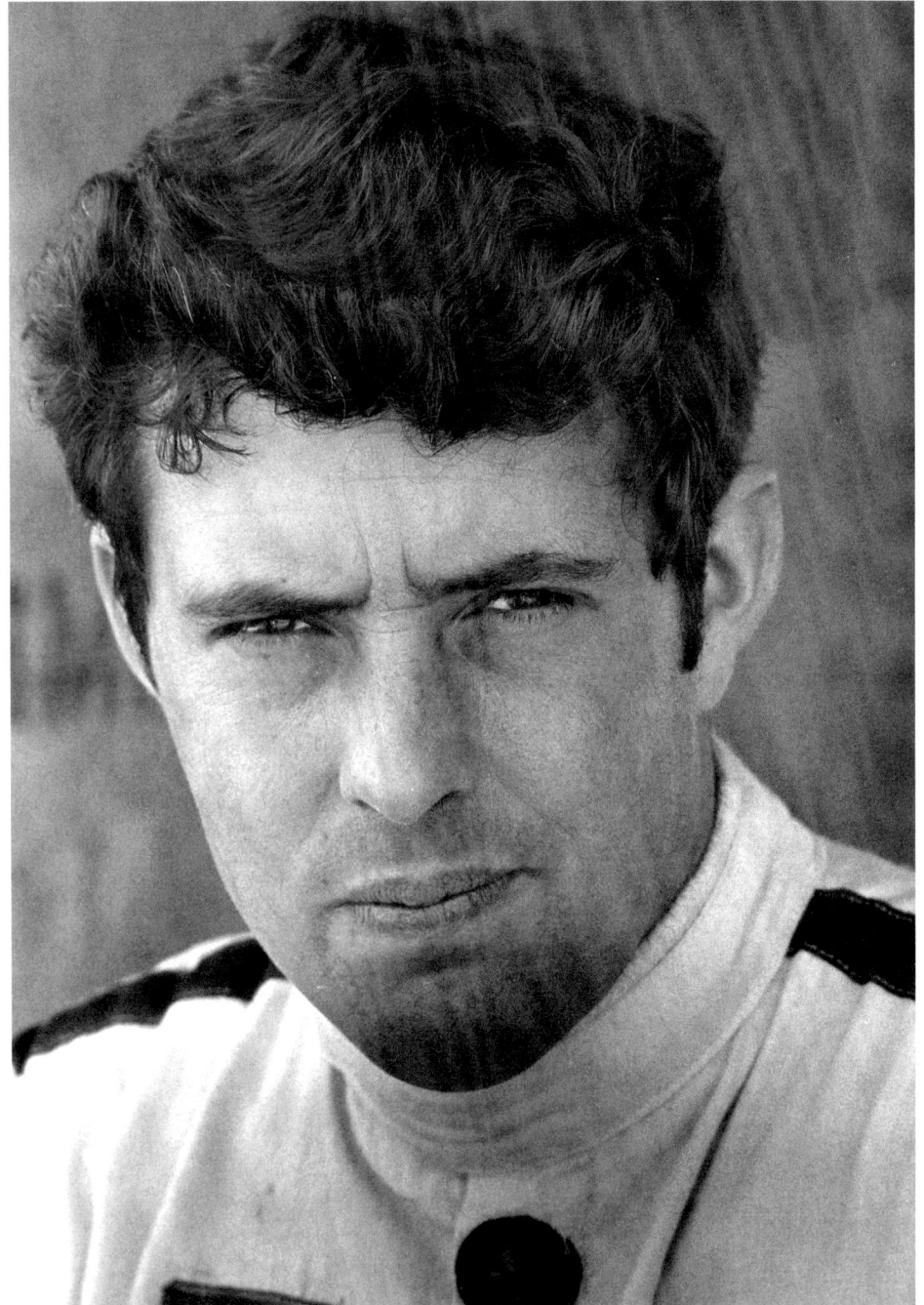

Brian Redman was another of the great Porsche drivers during the late 1960's and early 1970's. Redman achieved tremendous success with these cars and his wonderful sense of humor endeared him to those around him.

In 1972, Redman drove a factory Ferrari 312, and won the 1000 Kms of Spa that year.

1968 was the year that the Chaparral 2G really showed its stuff at the Bridgehampton Can-Am. After a bad start, Hall passed all of the front runners and was on his way to victory when he was forced to slow with fuel injection problems. Hall still finished second to Mark Donohue. Later in the year at Las Vegas, Hall and his Chaparral were involved in a spectacular accident that effectively finished Jim's driving career.

Jim Hall, one of racing's greatest innovators, and one of its most underrated drivers.

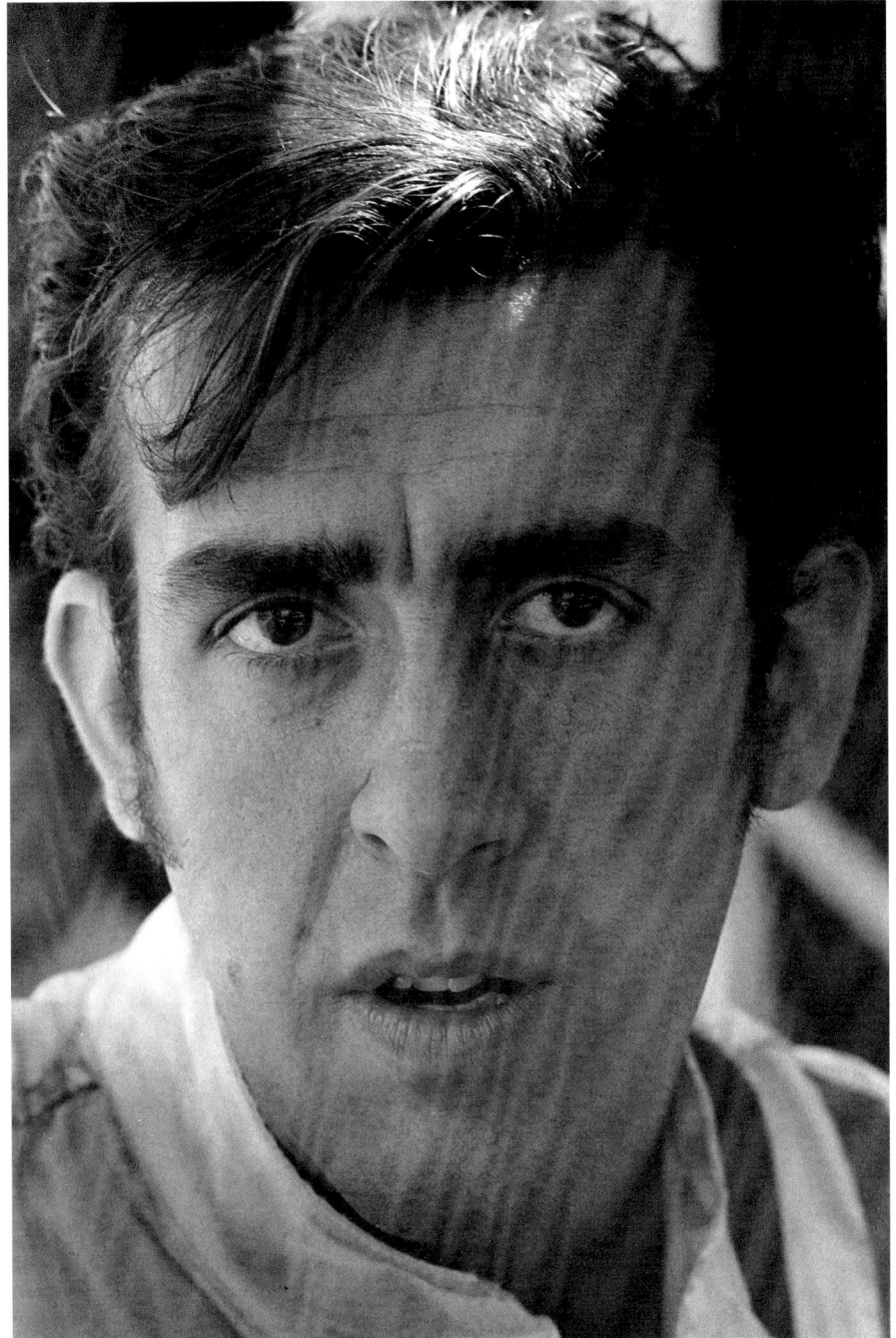

David Hobbs was also another of the sport's great characters. Hobbs was one of Europe's best all around drivers, driving everything from sports cars to Indy cars. He won the North American F5000 title in 1971.

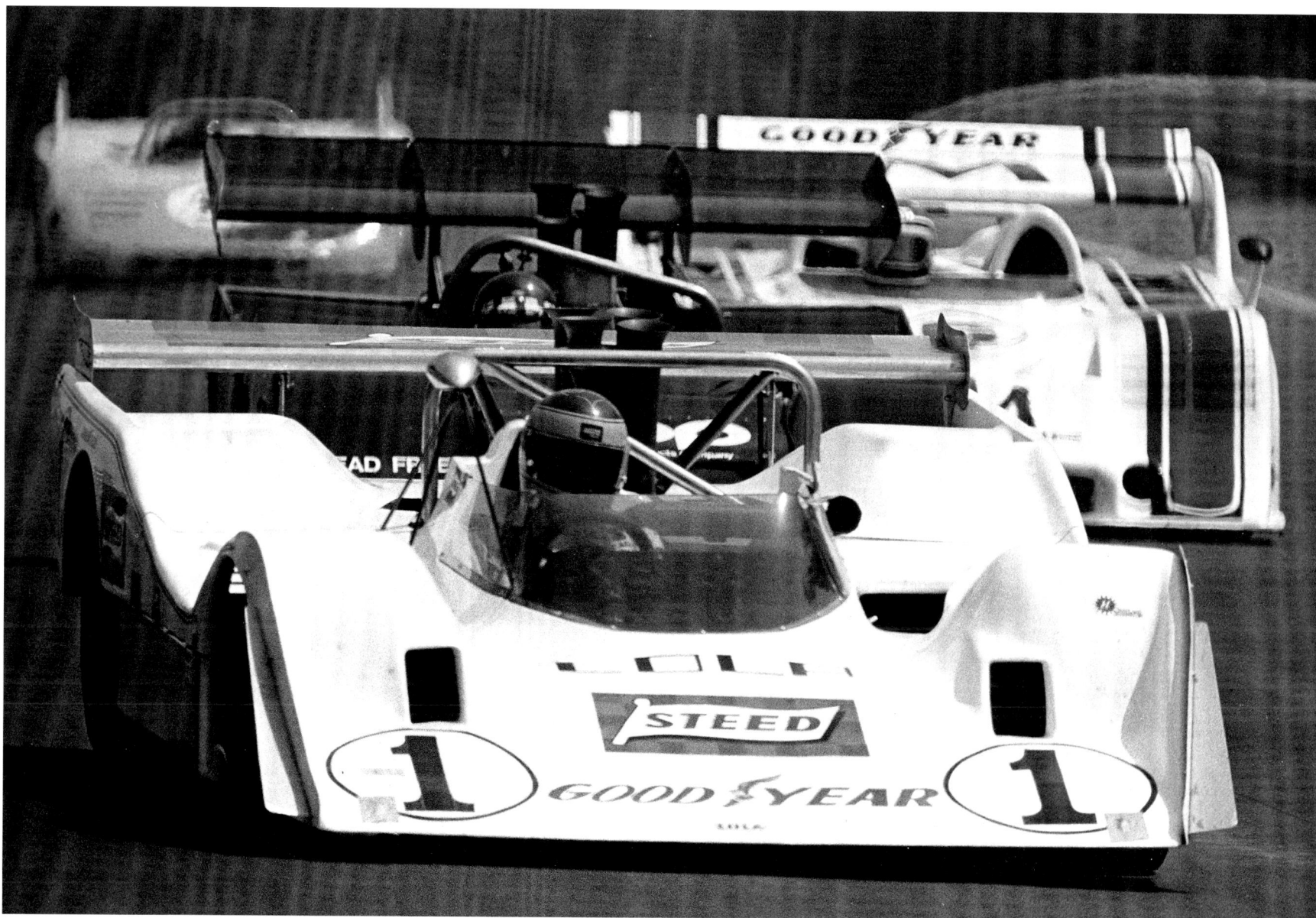

In 1972, Hobbs drove the radical Steed Lola T310 for Carl Haas in the Can-Am series. The car was plagued with problems and did not perform up to expectations.

Lothar Motschenbacher crests the hill at the 1971 St. Jovite Can-Am. Motschenbacher was the Trojan-McLaren representative at the time and always received the McLaren team cars at the end of the season.

Motschenbacher was known as "The Can-Am Ironman" because of his record of starting every Can-Am race from 1966 until he was injured in 1973. He was also famous for his beautifully prepared cars and his consistent high finishes.

Carroll Shelby celebrates one of the final wins of his career at Continental Divide Raceway in August, 1960. Shelby won the USAC Sports Car title that year and retired from the driver's seat to team ownership due to heart problems.

Shelby in his only appearance in the famous Meister Brauser Scarab. He drove the car to a win at the Continental Divide USAC race in August, 1960.

Jim Hall checks the position of the wing on the
Chaparral 2G prior to the start of the Riverside
Can-Am in October, 1968.

Innes Ireland, minus the nose of his Lotus 19, continues to press on at Mosport in September, 1962. Ireland finally had to retire from the race due to additional damage to the car.

George Follmer—Can-Am Champion 1972—USRRC Champion 1965.

In 1967 Can-Am events, Roger Penske offered George Follmer a ride in his spare Sunoco Lola T70. Penske had been impressed by Follmer's earlier season performances, and George responded with several well placed finishes during the series.

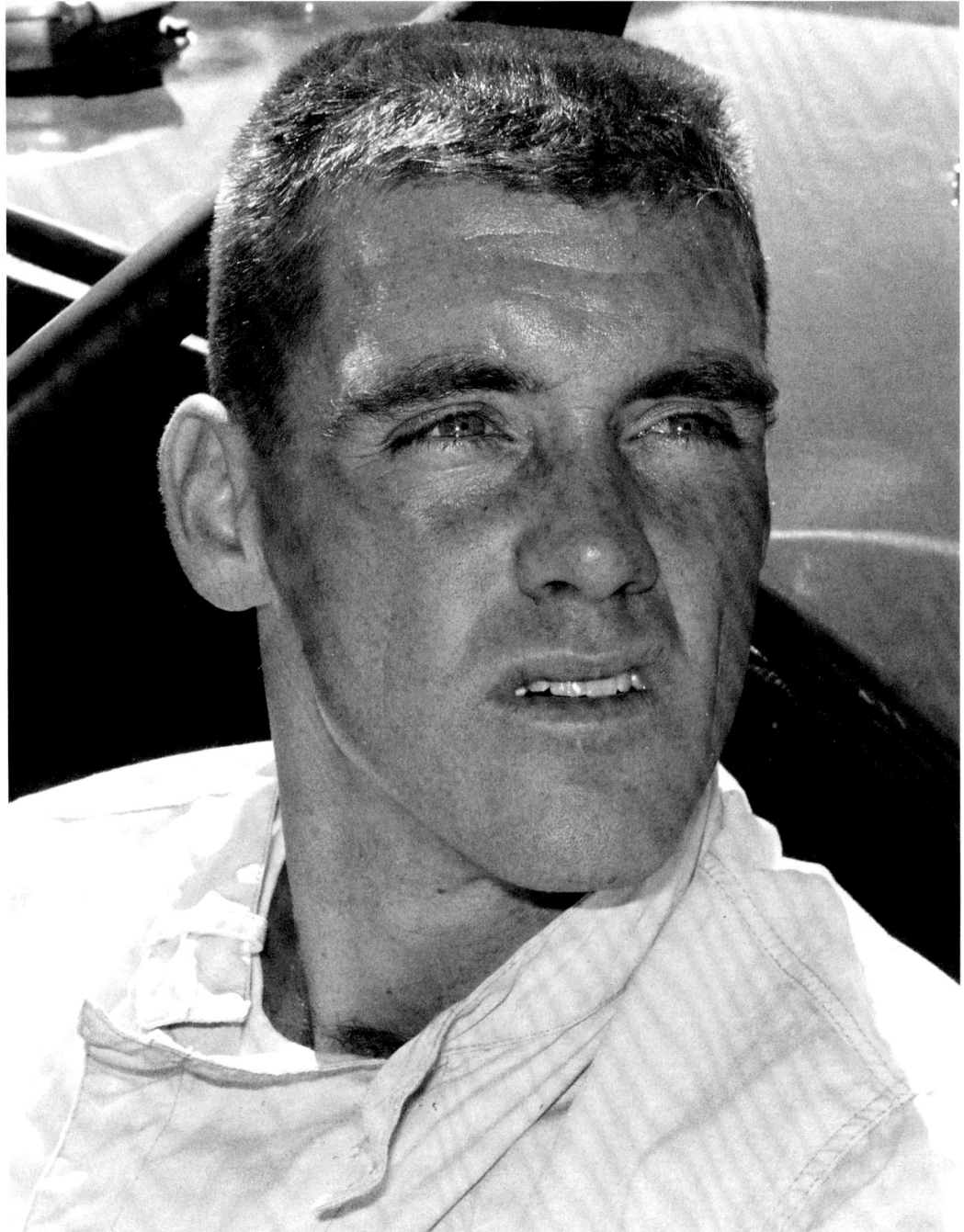

Dave MacDonald was one of racing's brightest rising stars during the 1963-1964 seasons. After joining the Shelby team in early 1963, MacDonald finally achieved the big time success that he deserved. Tragically, MacDonald was killed in a fiery accident at the Indianapolis 500 in May, 1964.

MacDonald achieved his greatest success by winning the two most prestigious professional sports car races in the world in October, 1963. Driving a Shelby American King Cobra, MacDonald won the Los Angeles Times Grand Prix at Riverside and the Pacific Grand Prix at Laguna Seca.

Bob Holbert was one of North America's most famous Porsche drivers. In early 1963, he joined Ken Miles and Dave MacDonald to form the formidable Cobra team. Holbert went on to win the first USRRC title in 1963 driving both a Porsche and a Cobra.

In 1964, Holbert was chosen to co-drive the new Cobra Daytona Coupe with Dave MacDonald. After retiring from the Daytona race due to a pit fire, the team won the Sebring GT class a month later. In May 1964, Holbert retired from racing after a serious accident at Kent, Washington.

John Surtees and...

Eric Broadley...

...brought to the world one of the most successful and
beautiful sports racing cars ever, the Lola T70. Surtees
won numerous races with this car from 1965 to 1967
and the first Can-Am championship in 1966.

Walt Hansgen—Laguna Seca, 1965.

Nino Vaccarella—Sebring, 1964.

Skip Hudson — Riverside, 1959.

Jo Siffert — Daytona, 1968.

Stirling Moss—Maserati Tipo 61—Sebring, 1960.

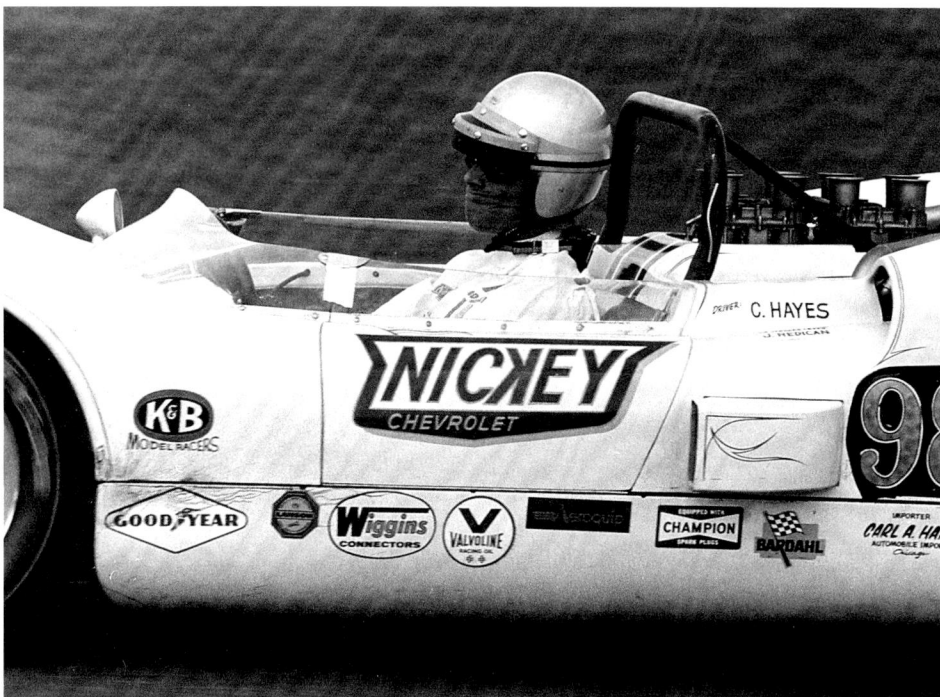

Charlie Hayes — McLaren M1A — Mid Ohio, 1966.

Denny Hulme — McLaren M6A — Las Vegas, 1967.

Chris Amon — McLaren M1B — Riverside, 1966.

Mike Spence — McLaren M1B — Las Vegas, 1967.

Jim Clark — Lotus 19 — Laguna Seca, 1963.

Bruce McLaren and Eoin Young enjoying the after race festivities at Nassau in December, 1964.

Roger Penske, driving a Chaparral 2, made his final season of driving a success by winning the 1964 Pacific Grand Prix at Laguna Seca. He became the only driver to ever win the three major races at the Nassau Speed Weeks.

Phil Hill in a car with which he had great success, the Ferrari TR59.

Looking more like a speedboat than a race car, the Chaparral 2 driven by Jim Hall and Hap Sharp scores a stunning win at the rain-swept Sebring 12 Hour in March, 1965.

Night comes and the crew of the Siffert/Hermann Porsche 907 rush to service the car in the shortest possible time.

Pedro Rodriguez leaps from his Ferrari TR61 during his pit stop at
the Canadian Grand Prix at Mosport, September, 1962.

Innes Ireland engages one of the 1962 Sebring officials in a rather heated exchange over the disqualification of the Ferrari that he and Stirling Moss were leading the race in. The problem occurred when Moss supposedly refueled two laps prior to the mandatory 20 lap period between fuel stops, however, the car was not disqualified until sometime later.

Denny Hulme and Peter Revson were McLaren teammates for the 1972 Can-Am series.

Seat in hand, Vic Elford is ready to take over the Porsche 907 from Jochen Neerpasch during the final hours of the 1968 Sebring 12 Hour race. Each driver had a special seat that was made for them so that the driver exchange could be made easier and faster by not having to do a lot of changes to the interior of the cockpit.

Jim Hall and Phil Hill were Chaparral teammates during the 1966 Can-Am series. Hill won the race at Laguna Seca for the only win ever by a Chaparral in Can-Am.

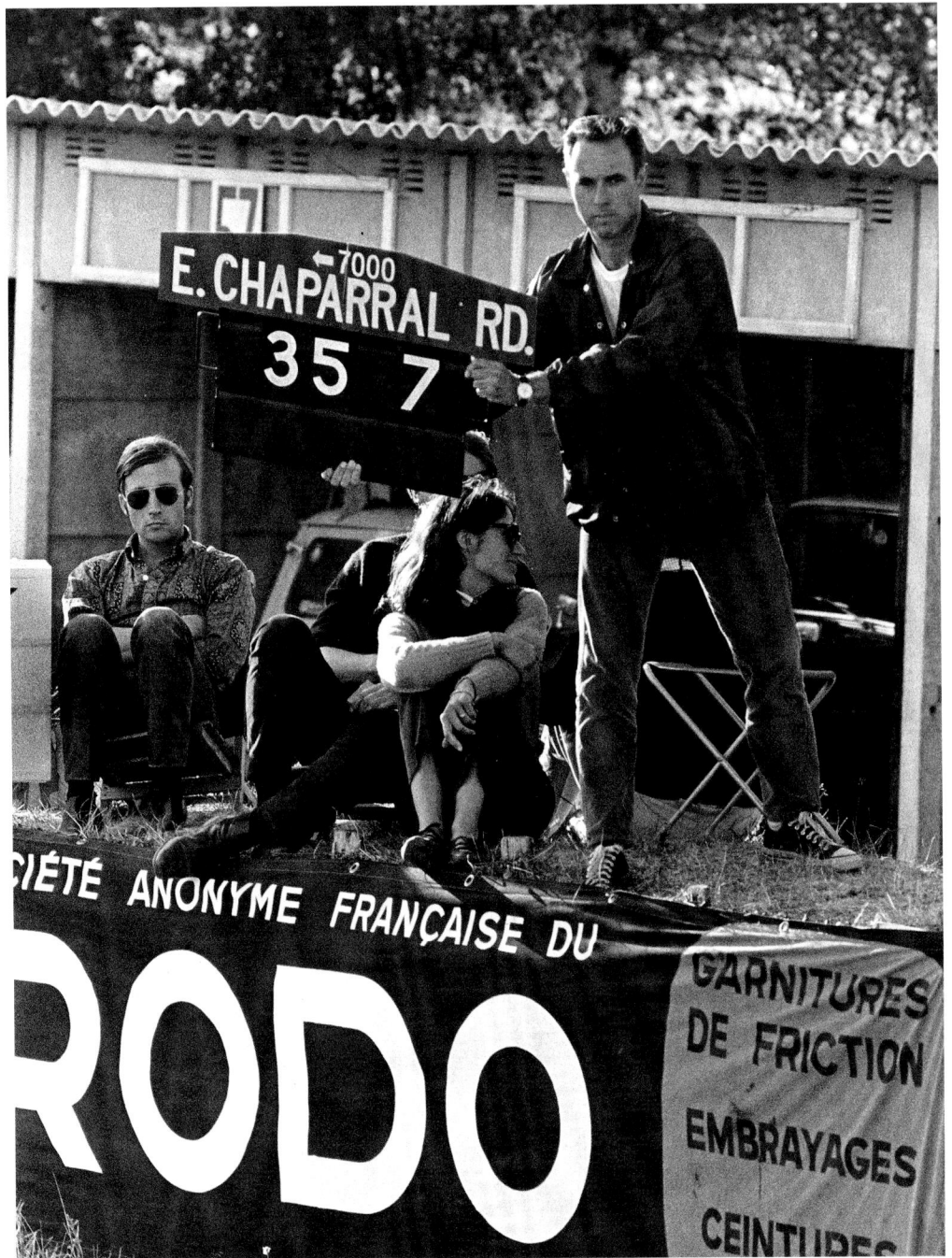

Chaparral signal station at LeMans in June, 1966.

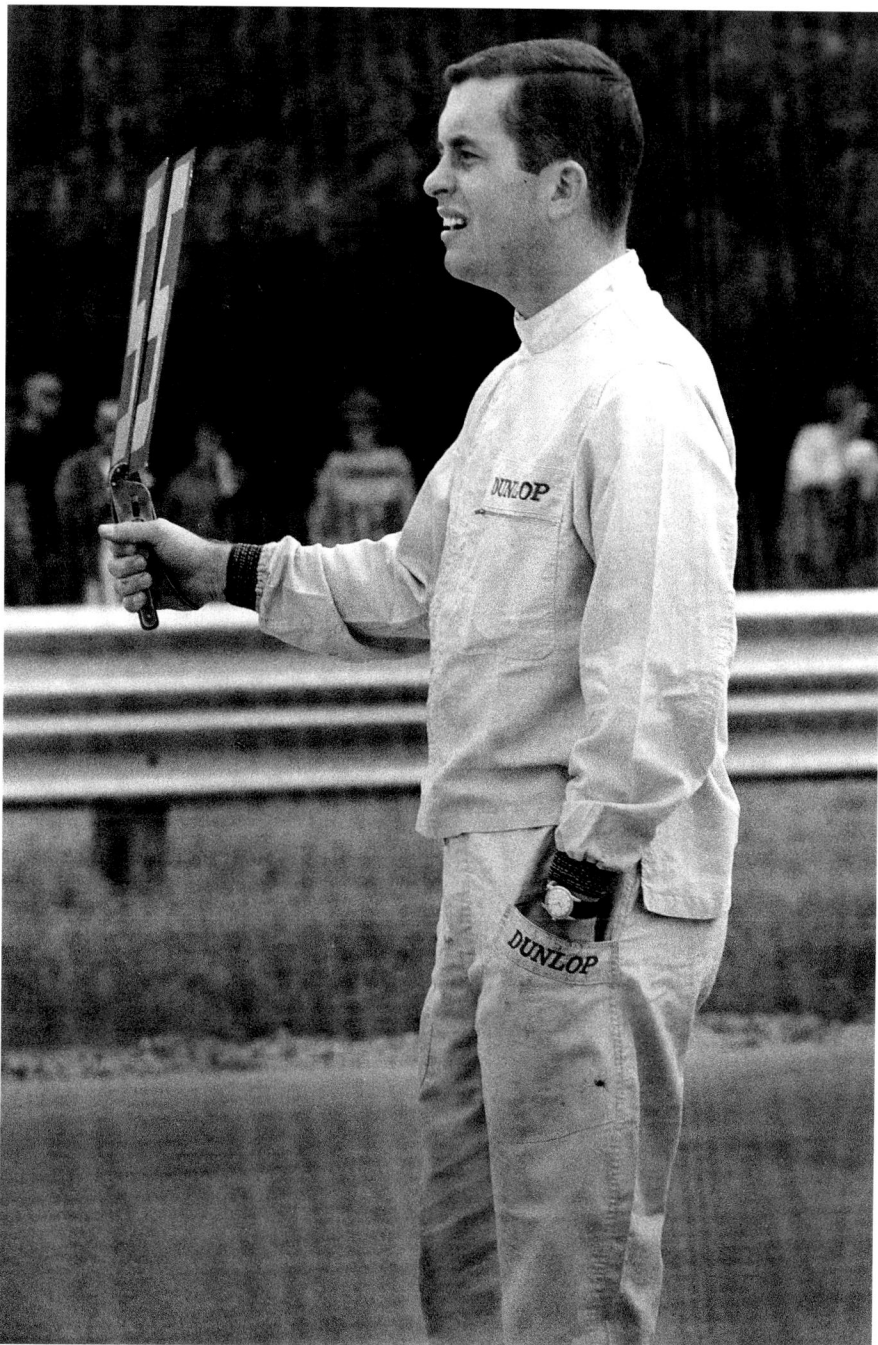

Roger Penske — Road America — September, 1962.

Brian Redman — Watkins Glen — July, 1970.

Denise McCluggage — Road America — September, 1965.

Famed car builder Max Balchowsky helps Dan Gurney's crew repair the transmission of Gurney's Lotus 19. When repairs could not be completed in the allotted time, Balchowsky offered Gurney his car, Old Yeller II.

New Zealand's three most famous drivers, Bruce McLaren, Chris Amon, and Denny Hulme, confer prior to the start of the 1969 Can-Am at Laguna Seca.

Augie Pabst, Walt Hansgen, and Briggs Cunningham—Laguna Seca—October, 1962.

Nina Rindt relaxes on the pit wall during practice for the 1967 LeMans 24 Hour.

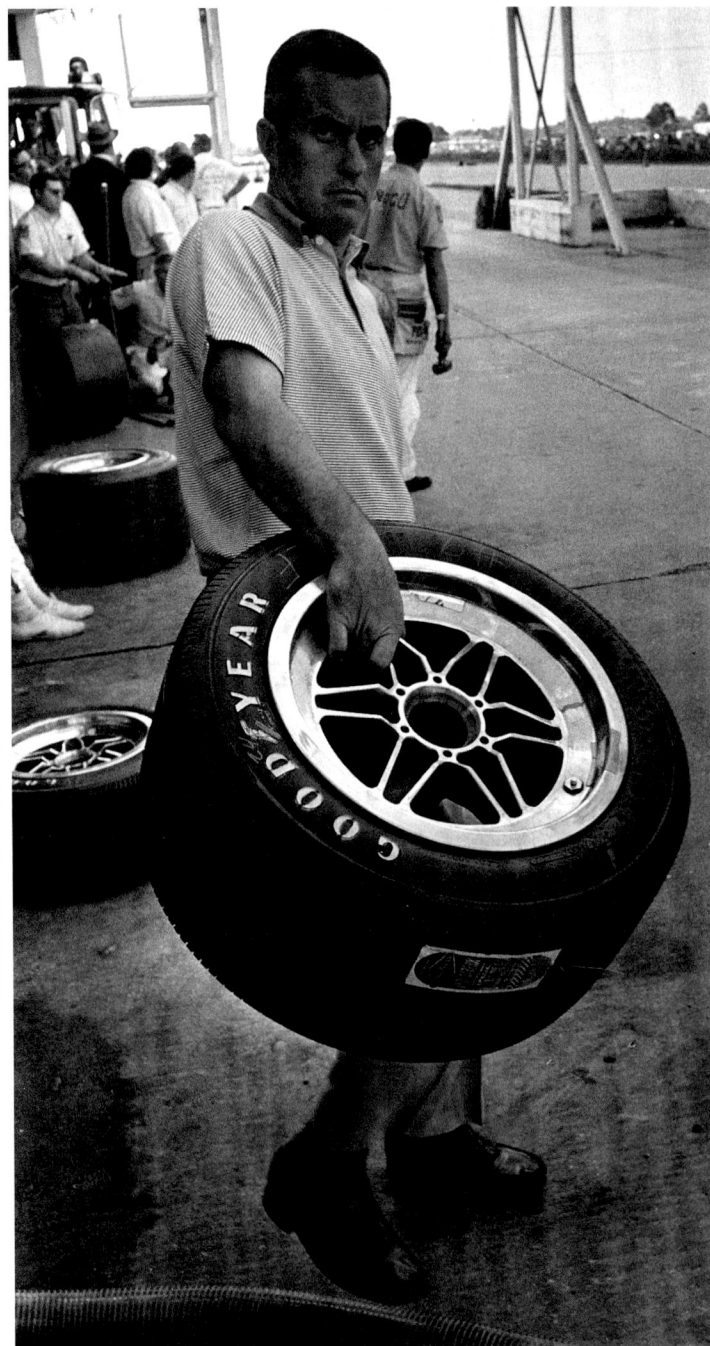

In the early days of Penske Racing, even the boss helped with the pit stops.

As Jim Hall gives Hap Sharp the OK sign during the 1962 Road America 500...

wife Sandy keeps the scoring and timing in order.

Bruce McLaren takes a moment to enjoy a Japanese car magazine during the 1968 Edmonton, Canada Can-Am. Note McLaren's chair.

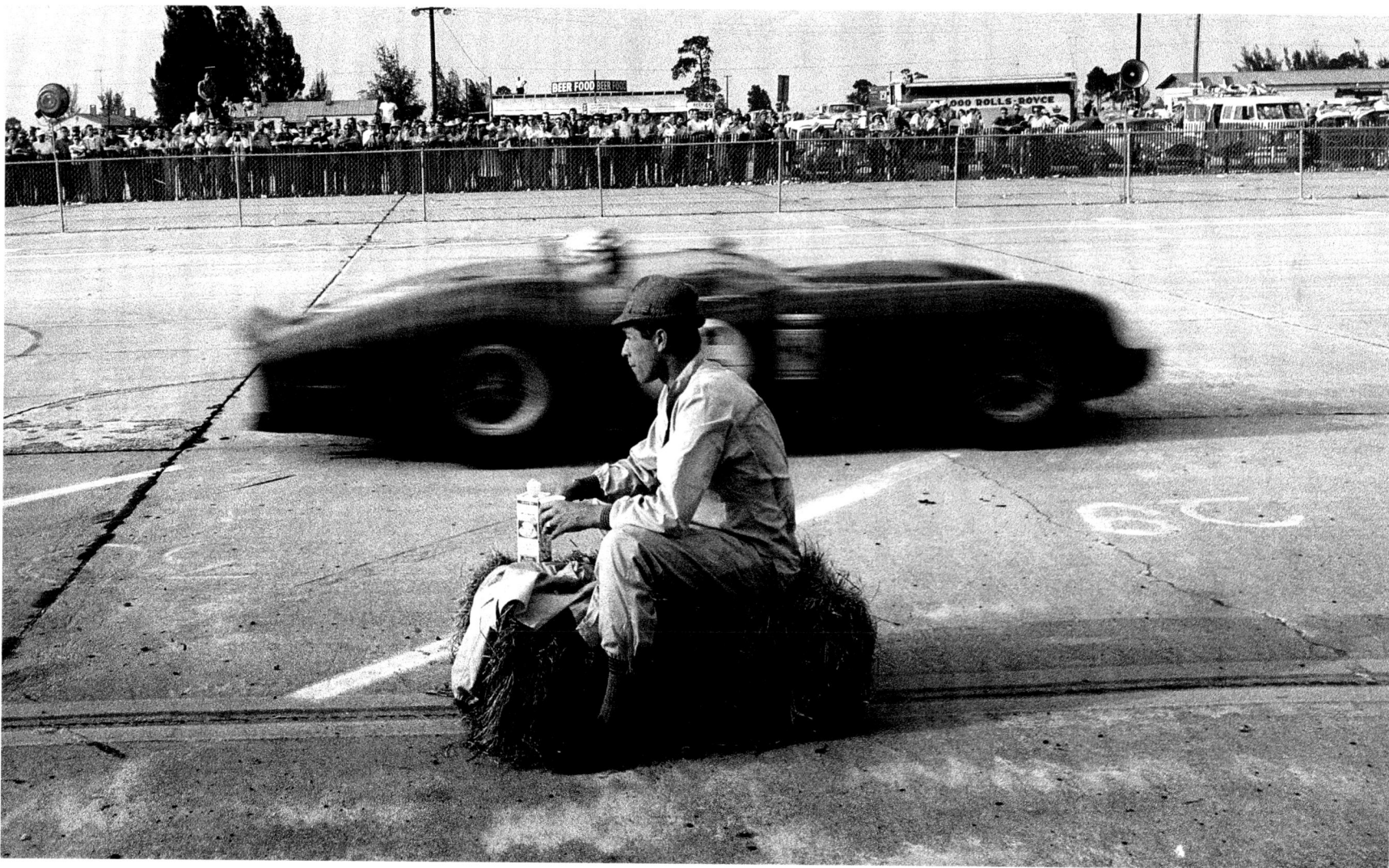

Not wanting to miss anything, Oliver Gendebien enjoys lunch from a strategic hay bale while Innes Ireland speeds by during the 1962 Sebring 12 Hour.

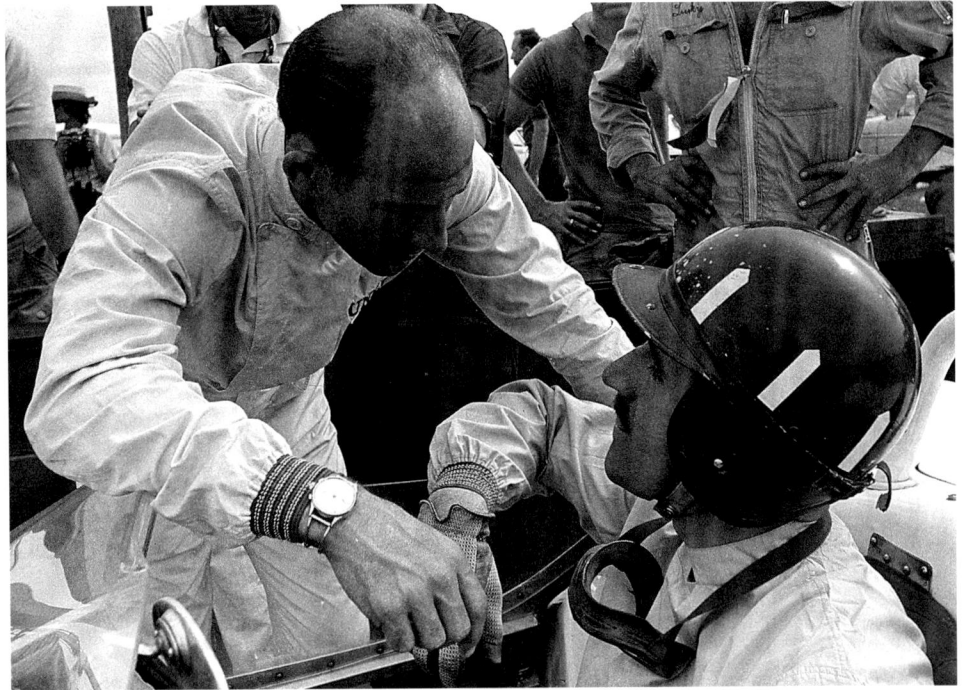

Stirling Moss and Graham Hill compare notes on the Maserati Tipo 61 they shared at Sebring, in 1961.

Vasek Polak and Wolfgang von Trips confer at Nassau in December, 1959.

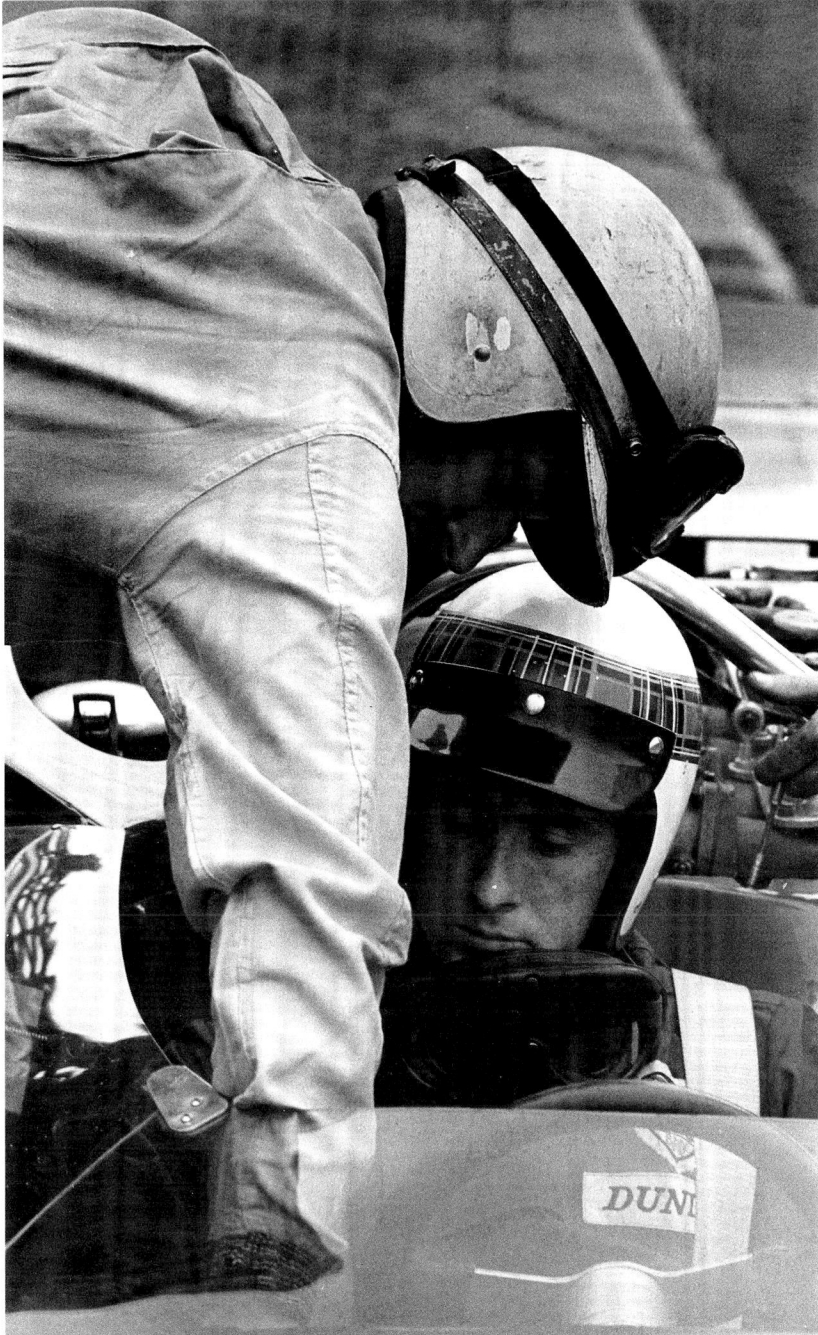

John Surtees makes a minor adjustment to Jackie Stewart's Lola T70 during practice for the 1965 Canadian Grand Prix at Mosport.

Dan Gurney and Ritchie Ginther at the start of the 1965 Sebring 12 Hour Race.

Ed Crawford pays the price for leaving the road at Sebring.

Roger Penske in his Zerex Special prior to the start of the Times Grand Prix in October, 1962. "Penske was responsible for bringing open rules sports car racing into being with his Zerex Special."

Charlie Agapiou and Wally Peat rush to complete an engine change in Augie Pabst's King Cobra at Mosport in June, 1964.

John Cooper—Sebring, 1962.

Ken Miles after the 1966 LeMans 24 Hour Race.

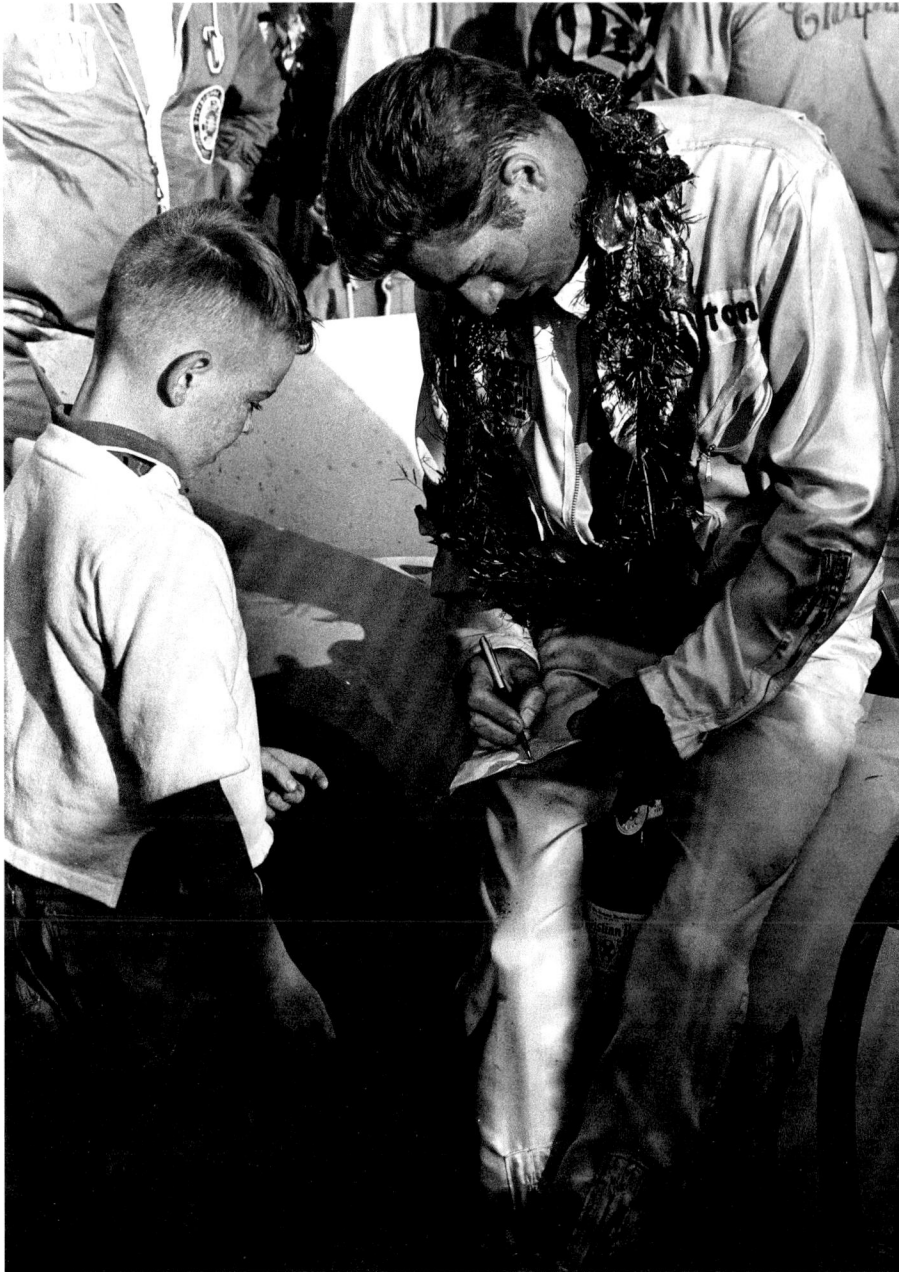

Jim Hall — Chaparral 2C — Kent, Washington — September, 1965.

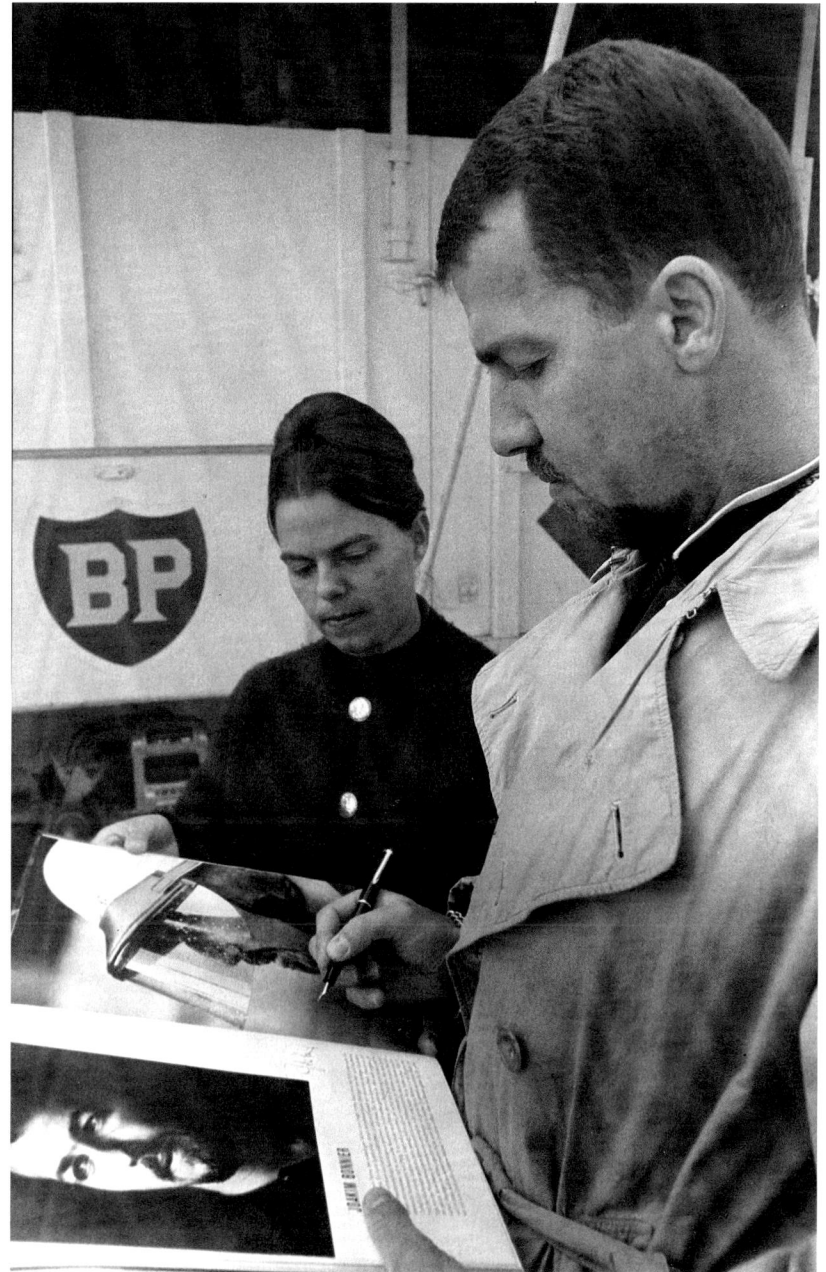

Jo Bonnier — Porsche Spyder — Mosport, Canada — September, 1962.

Steve McQueen was one film star who could have been an international racing star if he had chosen to go that route. McQueen and Peter Revson nearly won the Sebring 12 Hour race in 1970 driving this Porsche 908.

Jackie Stewart — Lola T70 — Mosport, Canada — June 1966.

Brian Redman enters the Gulf-Porsche 917K that he and Jo Siffert shared at the Watkins Glen 6 Hour Race in July 1970. These cars, under the direction of John Wyer, set a standard of excellence for other teams to follow.

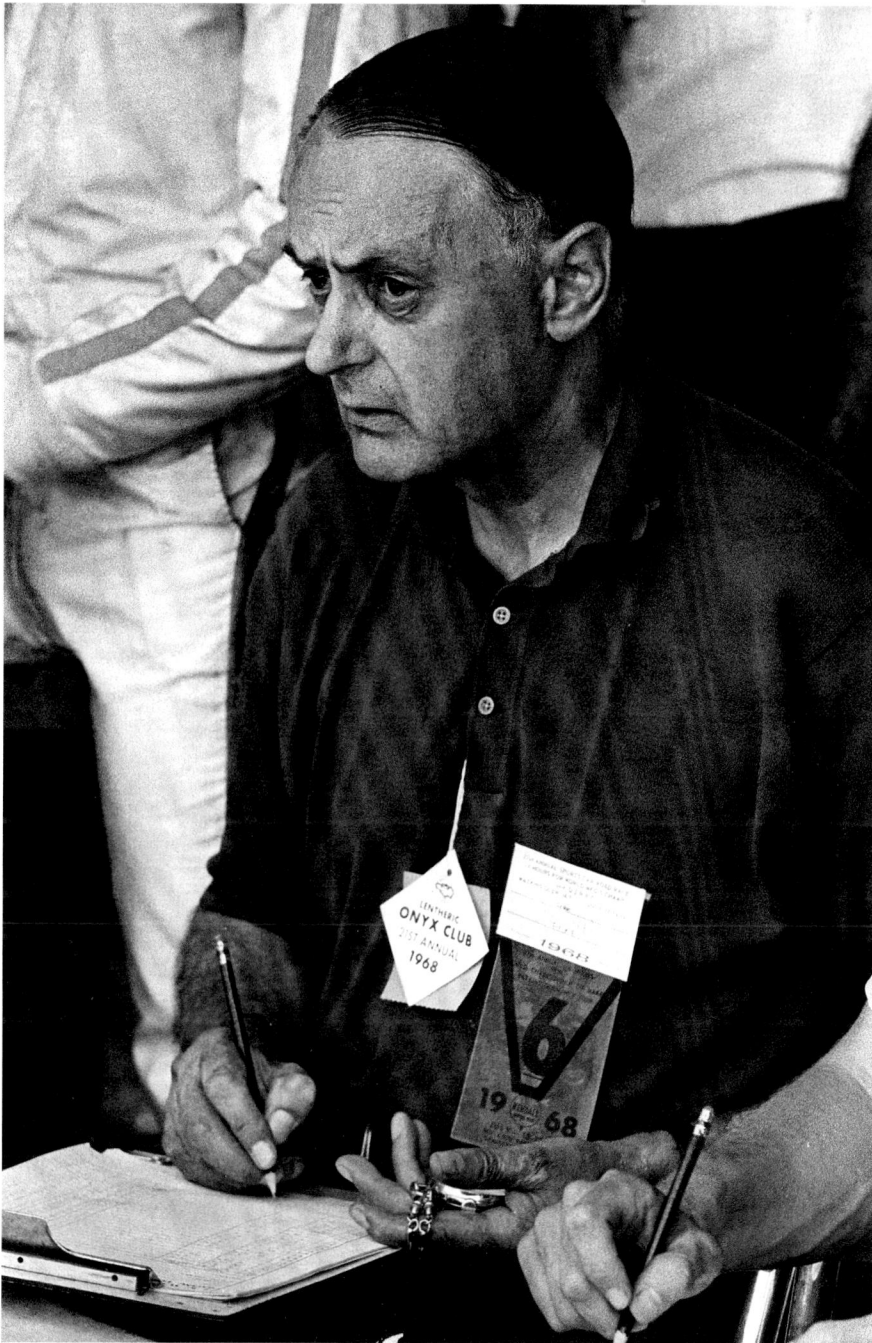

John Wyer was, most certainly, one of the finest team managers of all time. Although he had been associated with other programs in the past, his leadership of the Gulf racing program was his finest achievement.

The Chaparral 2J was the most radical and innovative car ever to appear in the Can-Am series. During the 1970 season, the car driven by Jackie Stewart and Vic Elford, set lap records wherever it ran. Unfortunately for everyone, the car was banned at the end of the 1970 season, in what Denny Hulme later described as "the biggest mistake ever made in the Can-Am."

Vic Elford was one of the greatest of the Porsche endurance drivers. His rally experience and photographic memory allowed him to learn a circuit faster than most others and gave him an advantage on many of the longer European courses.

Stirling Moss thrilled California race fans with his brilliant driving of the UDT Laystall Lotus 19. During the 1960-1961 seasons, he led every race he ran and won the Pacific Grand Prix at Laguna Seca in both 1960 and 1961.

Jody Scheckter was one of racing's rising stars when he drove the Vasek Polak Porsche 917/10 during the 1973 Can-Am season. Scheckter was soon to become a top notch Grand Prix driver and won the world championship for Ferrari in 1979.

Ford GT40 #1075 had a race record during the 1968-69 season that has never been matched. In 1968, the car won the BOAC 500, Spa, LeMans, and Watkins Glen. In 1969, it won Sebring and became the first car to ever win LeMans twice in a row.

Another car with a record that can never be matched was the McLaren M8B. In the 1969 Can-Am series, Bruce McLaren and Denny Hulme won all 11 of the Can-Am races with this, the best McLaren sports car ever built.

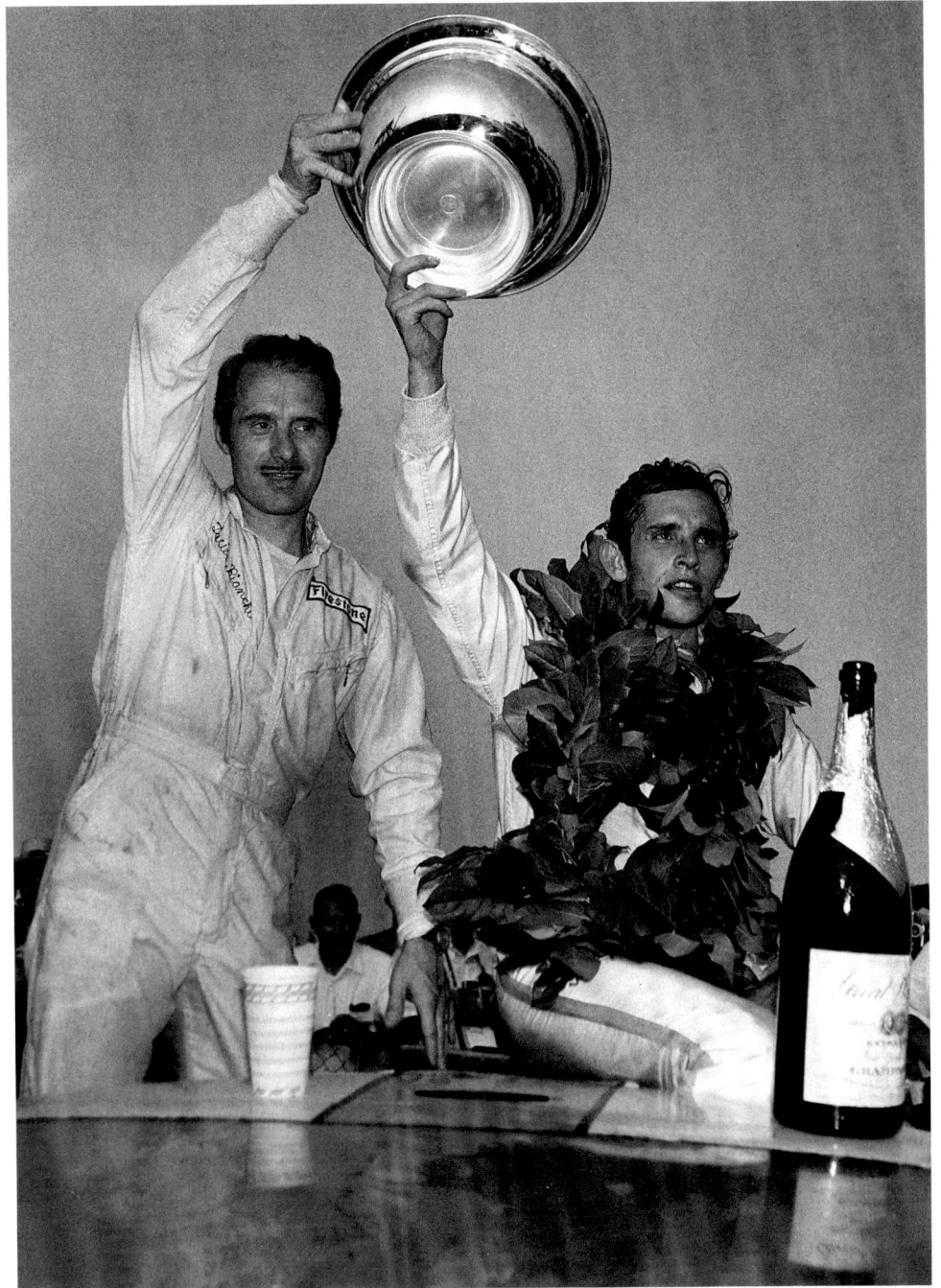

Lucien Bianchi and Jacky Ickx — Ford GT40 — Watkins Glen — July, 1968.

Dan Gurney—Lola T70—Bridgehampton—
September, 1966.

Jack Brabham — Cooper Monaco — Riverside —
October, 1961.

Innes Ireland — Lotus 19 — Nassau — December, 1962.

Jackie Stewart—Lola T260—St. Jovite—July, 1971.

Mario Andretti—Ferrari 512—Sebring—March, 1970.

A.J. Foyt wins the 1964 Indianapolis 500 and gives the front engined roadster its last win there.

CHAMPIONSHIP CARS

My first experience with the USAC Championship Cars happened at the Sacramento 100-mile dirt car race in October, 1960. What an experience! All of the great drivers of the era broadsliding through the corners wheel-to-wheel, rooster tails of dirt being thrown 50 feet into the air, and cars getting airborne as they slid across the ruts dug into the track by the power of the bellowing Offy engines. That was the era of narrow wheels, flimsy rollbars, and hard driving, hard drinking men. This was a special era that died in 1970 when the dirt tracks were dropped from the overall USAC championship.

I wish that my busy schedule during that time had allowed me the chance to attend more of the dirt races. It did, however, allow me to attend the Indianapolis 500 and a number of the road races for many years.

The great change at Indianapolis began in 1961 with Jack Brabham's Cooper and was, in my opinion, the speedway's most colorful era. This was a time when the great drivers from both sides of the ocean went nose-to-nose in some of racing's most memorable moments. It was an era that saw the beautiful, sleek roadsters and the powerful, evil-handling Novis disappear from the scene in favor of the smaller, faster, and better handling rear-engine cars. It was also a time when the STP Turbine cars dominated the 1967 and 1968 races and would have won except for some late race bad luck.

For many years, the championship races were run on dirt or paved ovals. It was during this period that more and more road races came into being and the ovals began to die out. Today, only five oval races remain on the championship schedule.

This was a wonderful time. It was a time of drivers like Foyt, Jones, Hurtubise, Ward, Andretti, Clark, Hill, and Stewart. It was a time of Offys, Fords, Chevys, Novis, and turbines. It was a time of narrow wheels and wide wheels, front engines and rear engines. Most of all it was an era of camaraderie among drivers and crews, and it was a time when a three-year-old car could come from the middle of the pack and win the race.

Photographically speaking, I especially remember shooting from the outside of the track, a practice hardly possible today, given all of the wire fencing and cement walls. For years, the best shots at Indianapolis were taken from the outside of the track entering and exiting the turns and in the short chutes. Very few photographers were brave enough — or stupid enough — to shoot from the outside at the dirt-car races. The cars would shoot dirt clods off their rear wheels that came at you like a missile attack. But if you were brave and could stand a little pain, the results were well worth it.

Colin Chapman and a jubilant Jim Clark waving to the crowd after winning the 1965 Indianapolis 500.

Jim Clark winning his first oval race at the Milwaukee 200 in August, 1963 driving a Lotus 29 Ford.

Graham Hill — Indianapolis 500 — May, 1966.

Mario Andretti and J.C. Agajanian — Hanford 150 — October, 1967.

Graham Hill — Indianapolis — May, 1966.

Lloyd Ruby — Indianapolis — May, 1967.

A.J. Foyt — Indianapolis — May, 1967.

Mario Andretti — Indianapolis — May, 1967.

A.J. Foyt and George Bignotti formed one of championship racing's most famous and successful driver-mechanic combinations. The Foyt-Bignotti combination won 27 championship races from 1960-1965.

Rodger Ward checking the fuel tank of his roadster before the 1962 Indianapolis 500. Ward won the race.

Jim Clark—Indianapolis 500—May, 1966.

Jim Clark winning the 1965 Indianapolis 500 in a Lotus 38 Ford.

George Follmer—Riverside—December, 1968.

266

One of the biggest upsets in oval track racing came at the Phoenix 150 in March, 1969. George Follmer, primarily known as a road racer, beat a field of the best oval track racers driving a car of his design and powered by a stock-block Chevy engine. This was the first championship win for a stock-block engine.

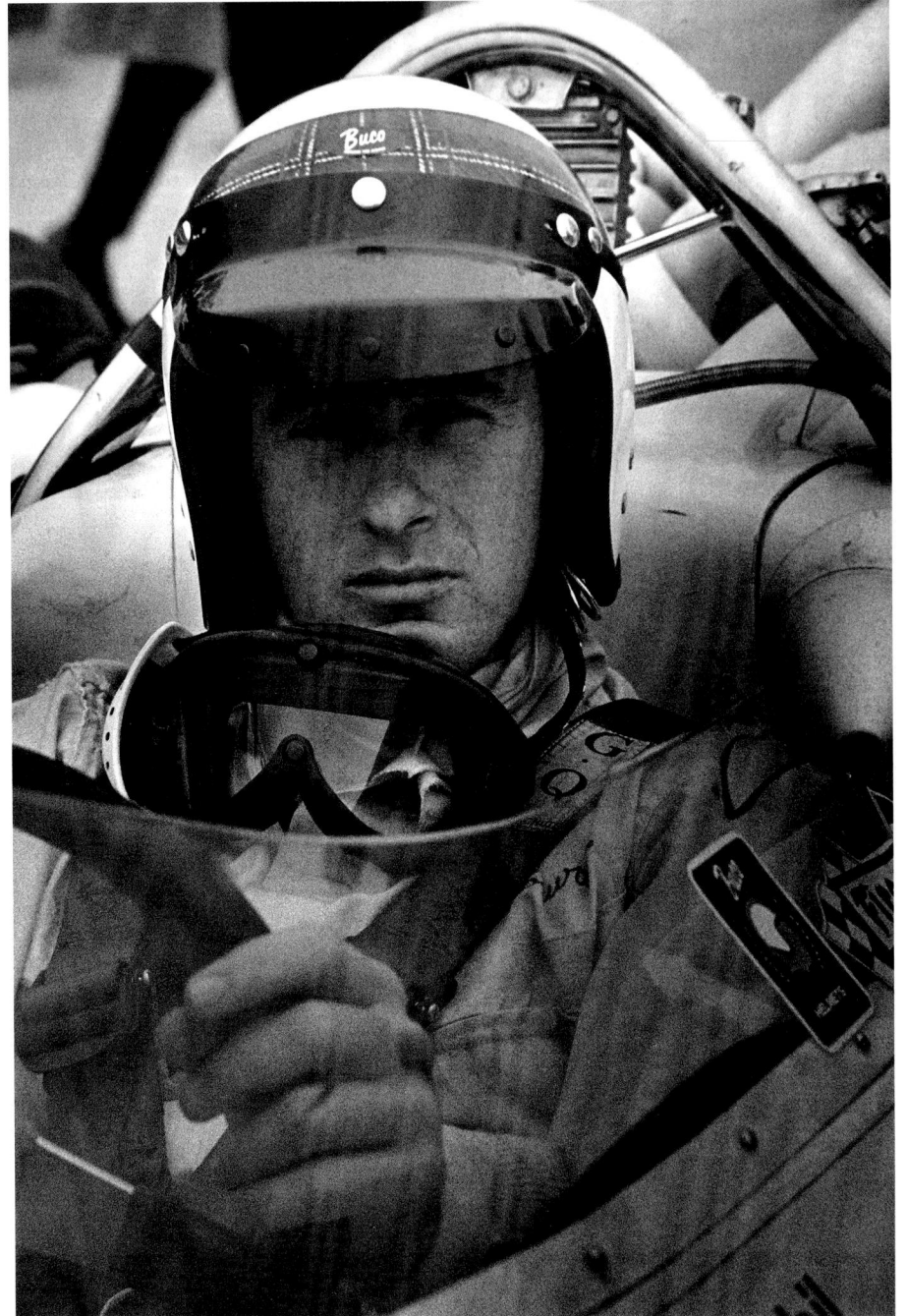

Jackie Stewart — Indianapolis — May, 1966.

Jackie Stewart making a smashing debut at the 1966 Indianapolis 500. Driving a John Mecom Lola-Ford, Stewart was near the front for the entire race and was leading with eight laps to go when engine failure put him out.

Mario Andretti — Indianapolis — May, 1967.

Andretti first arrived at the speedway in 1965 and finished third. Since then Mario has set numerous track records and was the winner of the 1969 race. Mario has won 51 championship races and four national championships during his long career.

Rodger Ward—Indianapolis—May, 1966.

On dirt or on pavement, Rodger Ward was a tough competitor. Before retiring at the end of the 1966 season, Ward won Indianapolis twice, a total of 26 championship races, and two national championships.

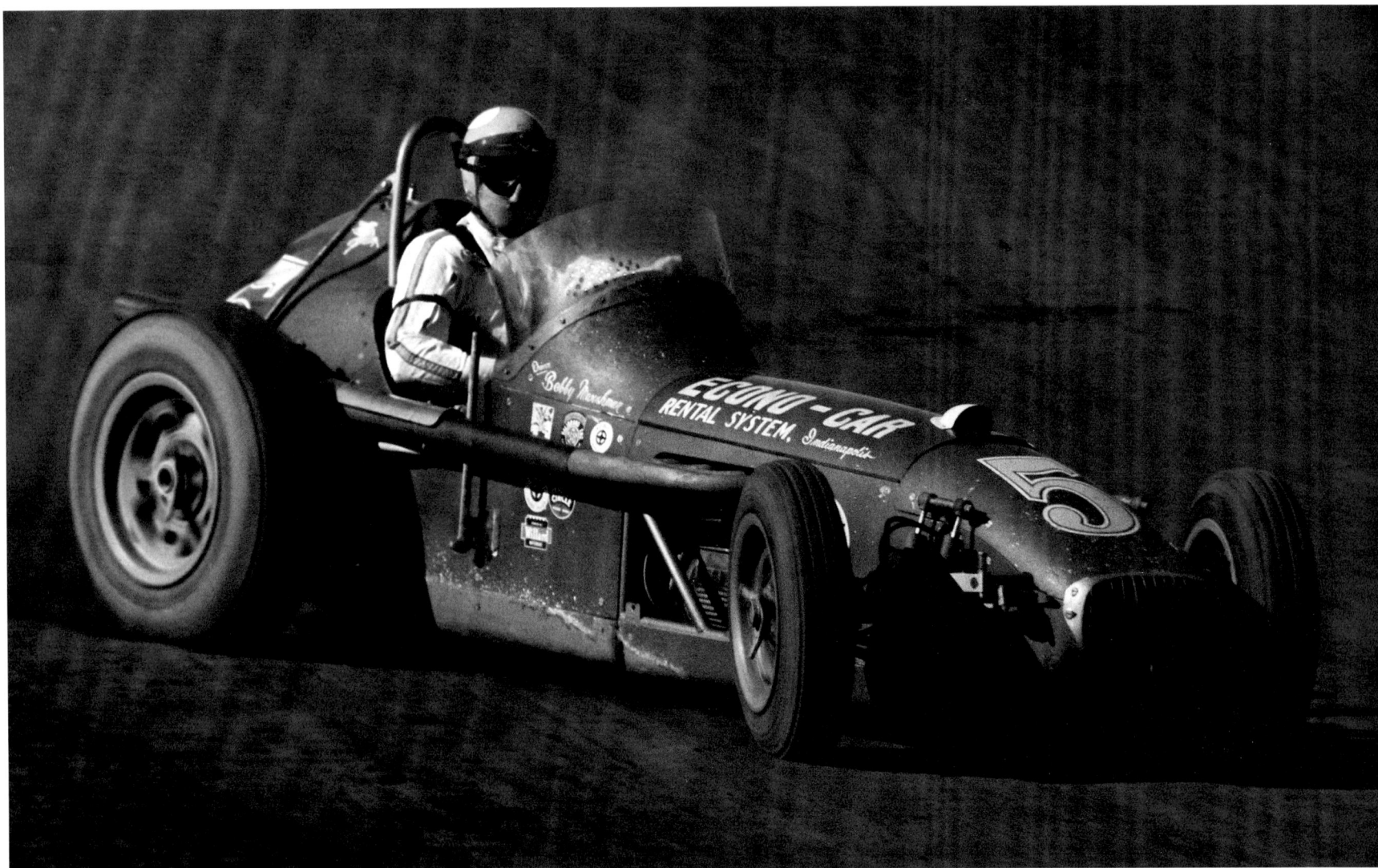

Although he won only one championship event during his brief career, Bobby Marshman was one of the top drivers on the circuit. Marshman was killed in a testing session at Phoenix shortly after the close of the 1964 season.

Bobby Marshman—Phoenix—November, 1964.

Joe Leonard came to car racing from motorcycles where he had won several national championships. During his 11 year career, Leonard won six championship races and two consecutive national championships.

Joe Leonard — St. Jovite — August, 1967.

Bobby Unser—Indianapolis—May, 1968.

Al Unser—Indianapolis—May, 1966.

Troy Ruttman — Indianapolis — May, 1964.

Jerry Grant — Indianapolis — May, 1964.

Bobby Unser—Indianapolis—May, 1964.

At Pikes Peak where he first made a name for himself or on the pavement where he recorded three wins at the Indianapolis 500, Bobby Unser always ran with the leaders. Unser won 35 championship races and two national championships before retiring in 1981.

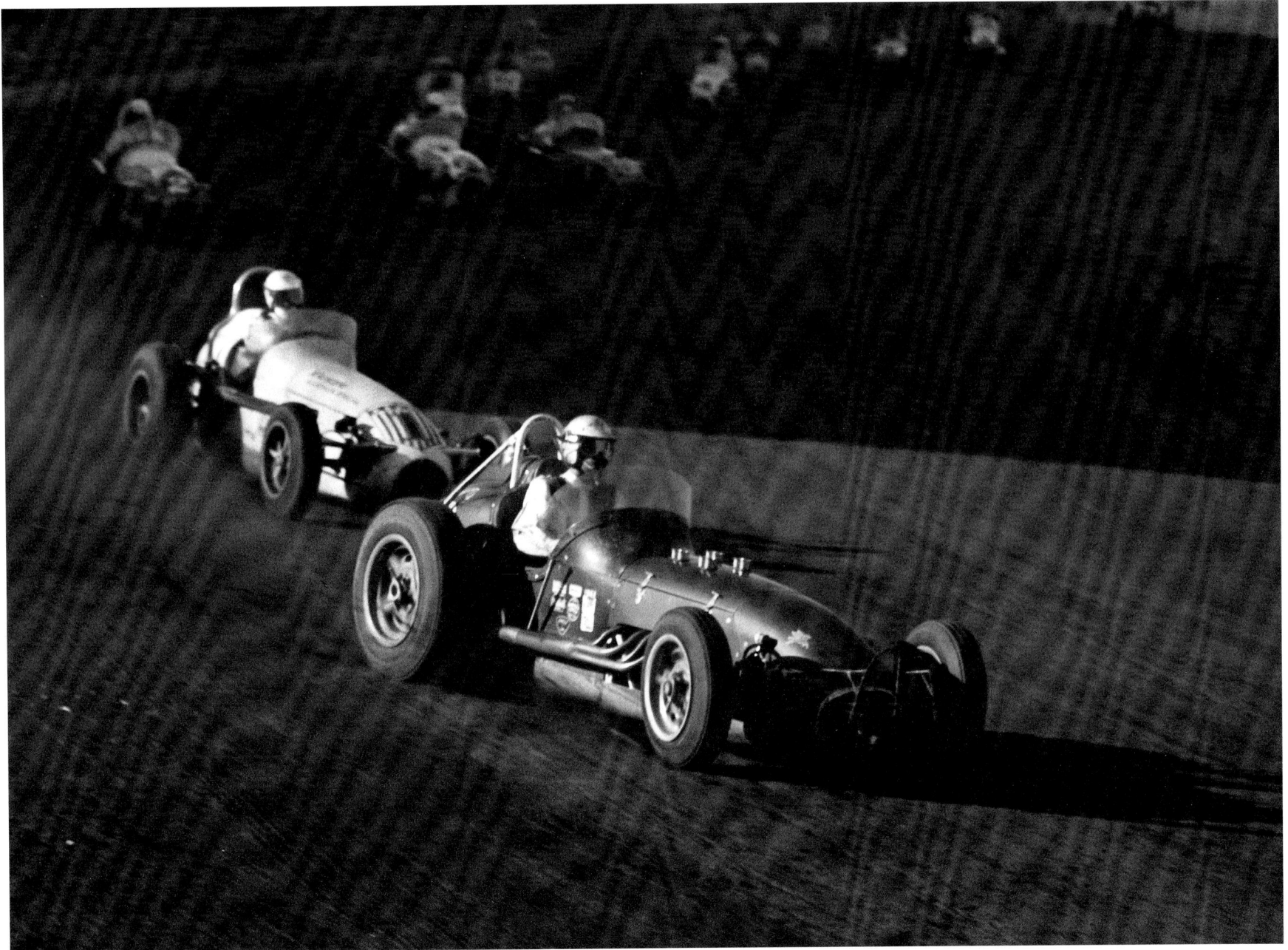

Johnny Rutherford came up through the ranks of the tough IMCA midwest sprint car organization. Rutherford proved he could win in the big time by winning the Indianapolis 500 three times, 27 championship wins, and a national championship over 30 years.

Johnny Rutherford — Phoenix — December, 1964.

285

One of the most important moments in Indianapolis history occurred when Rodger Ward talked Jack Brabham and John Cooper into bringing one of their rear engined Formula One cars to the 1961 Indianapolis 500. Although the car was underpowered, Brabham finished ninth and the rear engine revolution was begun.

Chief Steward Harlan Fengler gives Brabham some advice regarding the speedway rules.

"Good Luck Jack From The Boys at Climax" is what the note accompanying the spare Cooper engine reads.

Danny Oaks working on the engine of the Demler Special. In May, 1963...

as George Bignotti heats up his Offy's block in May, 1964.

Jim Clark seems more interested in the art on the wall than on what's being done to his Lotus 38.

This Offy engine, or what's left of it, demonstrates the meaning of the racing term, sawed in half.

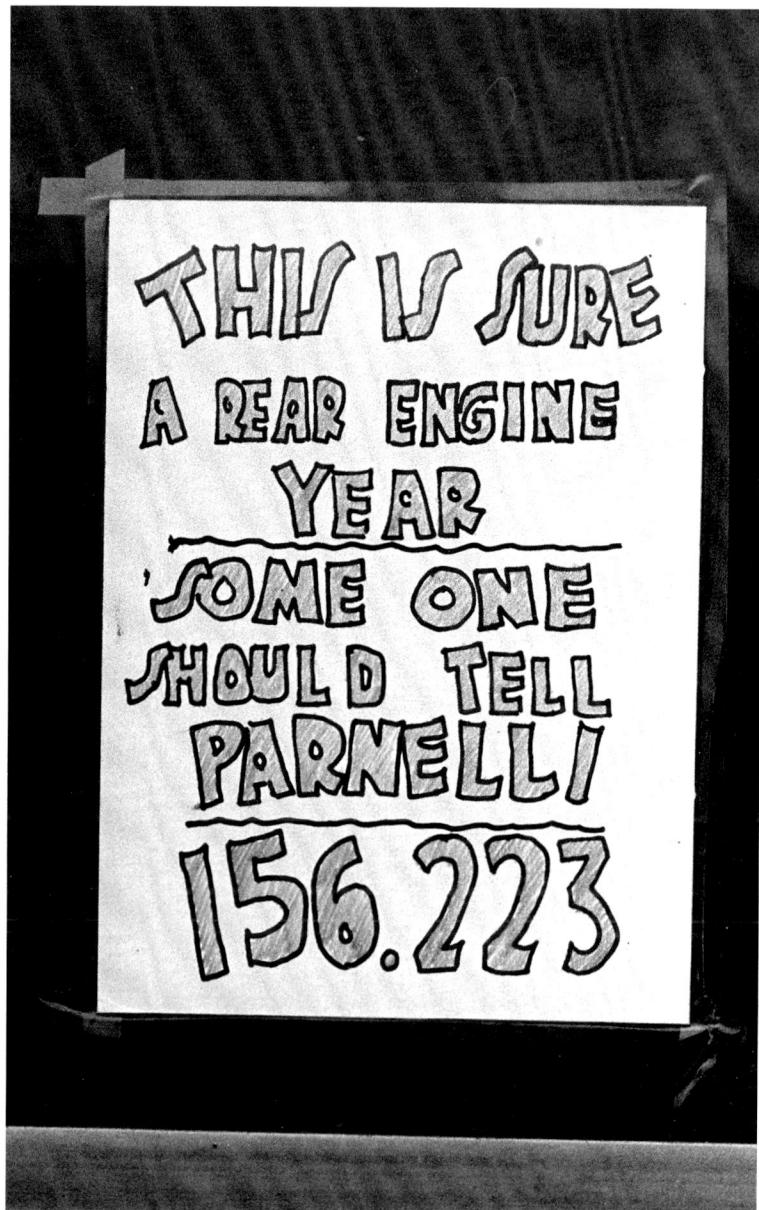

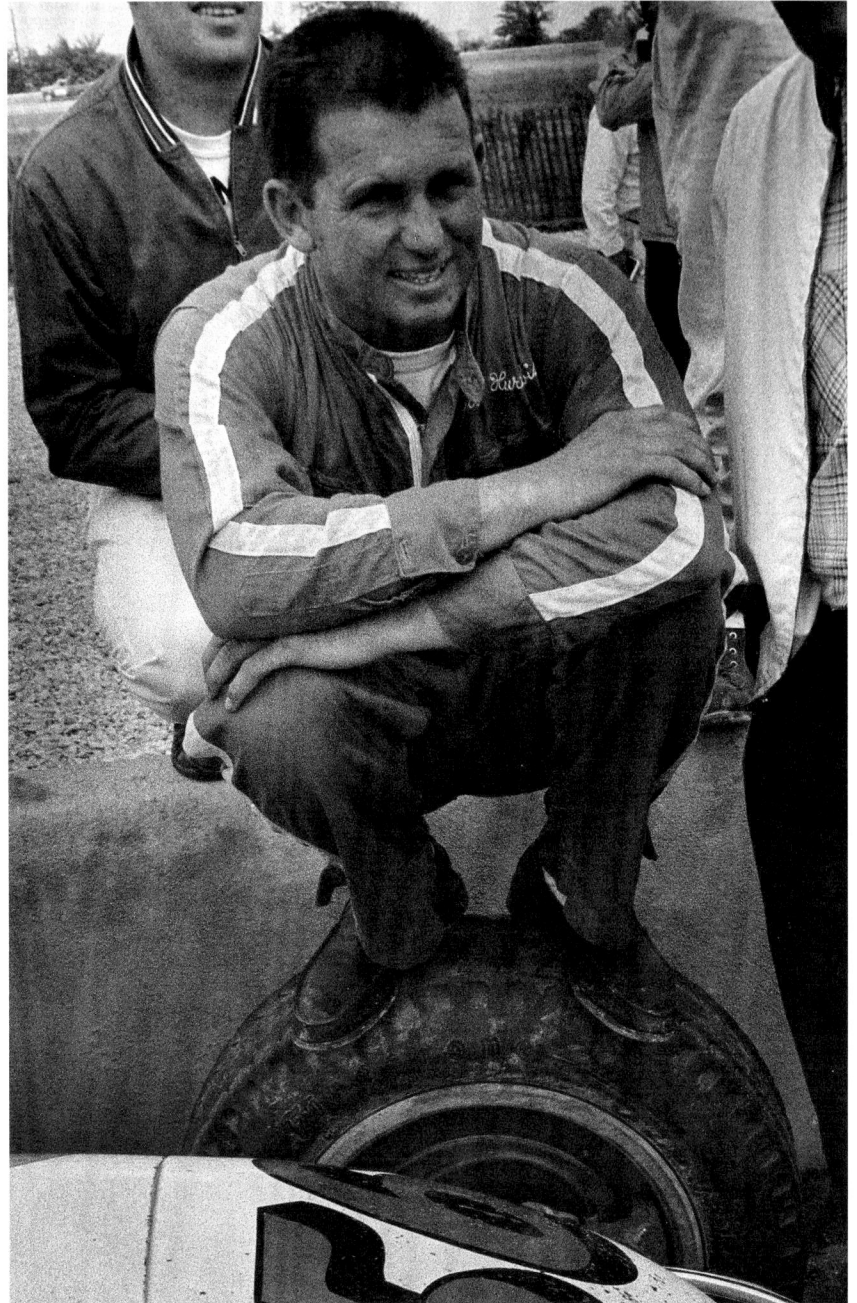

One of racing's hardest chargers and one of its greatest pranksters, Jim Hurtubise, was most at home on the dirt tracks. His famous #56 Sterling Plumbing Special was always near the front and he never let the crowd down for lack of excitement.

Parnelli Jones was another of the drivers who came up through the tough sprint car ranks. His races with A.J. Foyt (#3 Konstant Hot Special) and Jim Hurtubise in the early 60's are still considered to be some of the greatest ever.

A.J. Foyt, the name says it all. Four Indianapolis 500 wins, 67 championship wins, and seven national championships. During the 1960's, Foyt was known to many as "the toughest man alive." Anyone who ever saw him on a one mile dirt track would never dispute that fact.

A.J. Foyt — Indianapolis — May, 1963.

Paul Goldsmith leads a group of front runners through the third corner of the 1963 Indianapolis 500. In the middle of the pack of front engined roadsters, one can see the tiny Lotus-Fords of Jim Clark (92) and Dan Gurney (93) about to make their move.

Jack Brabham—Indianapolis—May, 1964.

Jim Rathmann, winner of the 1960 Indianapolis 500, leads Len Sutton at the 1963 Indianapolis 500.

Parnelli Jones and "Silent Sam" the turbine powered STP-Paxton Turbocar of Andy Granatelli that rocked the 1967 Indianapolis 500 to its foundation. After qualifying sixth, Jones passed all of those in front of him on the first lap and set sail. Jones led almost the entire race until 4 laps from the finish when a small transmission part broke, putting him out of the race.

Dan Gurney and Mark Donohue battle for the lead at the 1968 Rex Mays 300. Gurney won two of the three Rex Mays races run at Riverside.

Parnelli Jones takes his final ride in "Old Calhoun" at the 1964 Indianapolis 500 before turning to the new rear engine cars. During the four years Jones drove this roadster, he became the first man to qualify for the race at over 150 mph and he finally won the race in 1963.

Mario Andretti (1), Bobby Unser (6), and Ronnie Bucknum (23) battle for the lead at the 1967 St. Jovite 200 mile race. Andretti in the Dean Van Lines Spl. won.

Roger McClusky—Las Vegas—April, 1968.

Mario Andretti—Phoenix—November, 1965.

Lloyd Ruby — Las Vegas — April, 1968.

A.J. Foyt — Phoenix — November, 1965.

Typical midget action of the era shows what happens when drivers get too close.

Another group of midgets, with A.J. Foyt (5) and Johnny Moorhouse (27) about to break out of the pack.

Norm Hall (14) Chuck Hulse (23), Parnelli Jones (98) lead pack of midgets at Ascot, February, 1963.

Parnelli Jones accommodates the autograph seekers. Note Rodger Ward's autograph on the open book.

The AAR crew of Dan Gurney celebrate Gurney's victory at the 1967 Rex Mays 300.

Clint Brawner of Dean Van Lines was one of racing's most successful and legendary mechanics.

Bob Wilke, owner of the Leader Card team was one of the era's most successful car owners.

Jackie Stewart seems to be telling Lucien Bianchi that he doesn't want to be in this position in one of the corners.

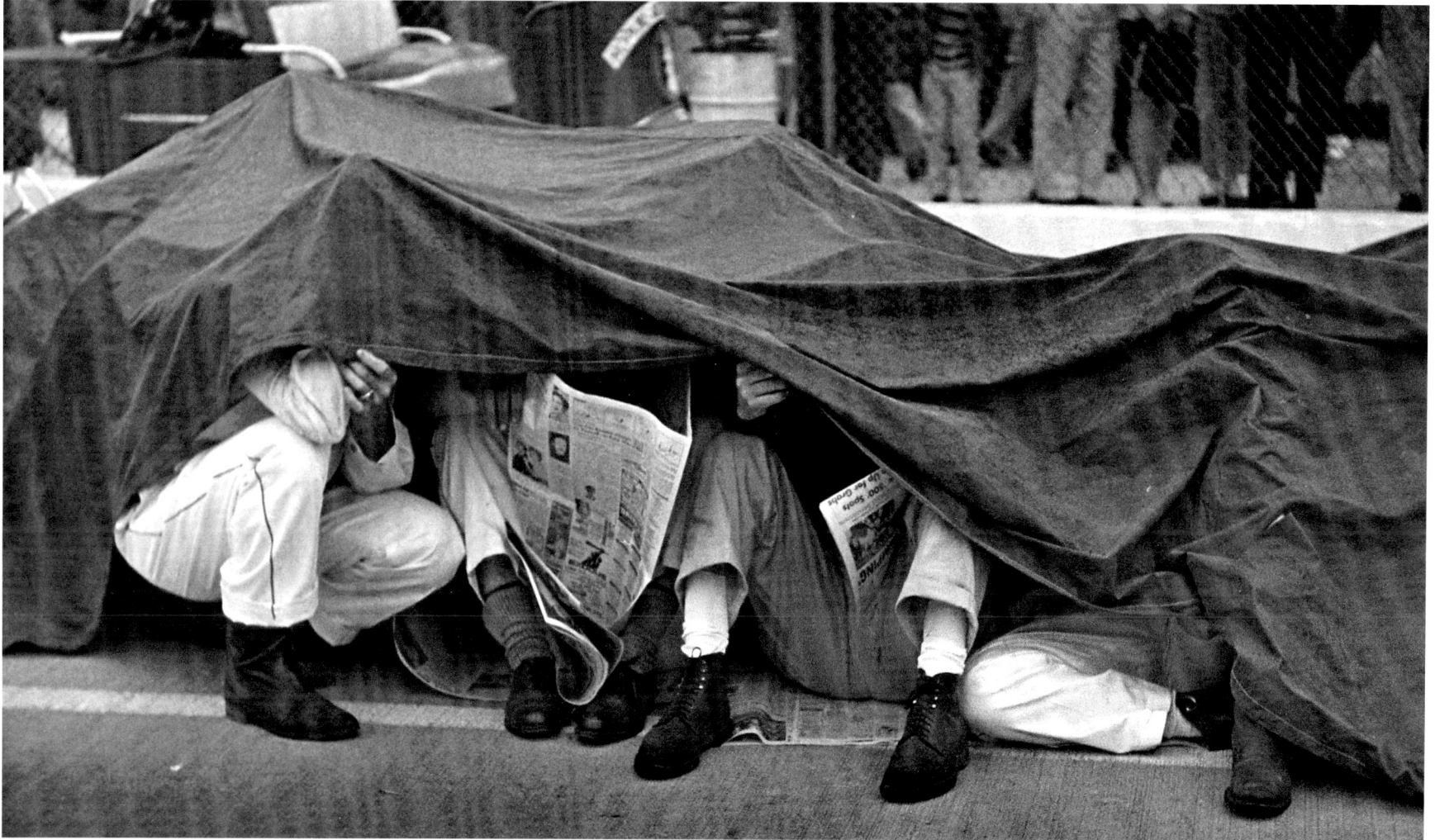

Waiting out the rain.

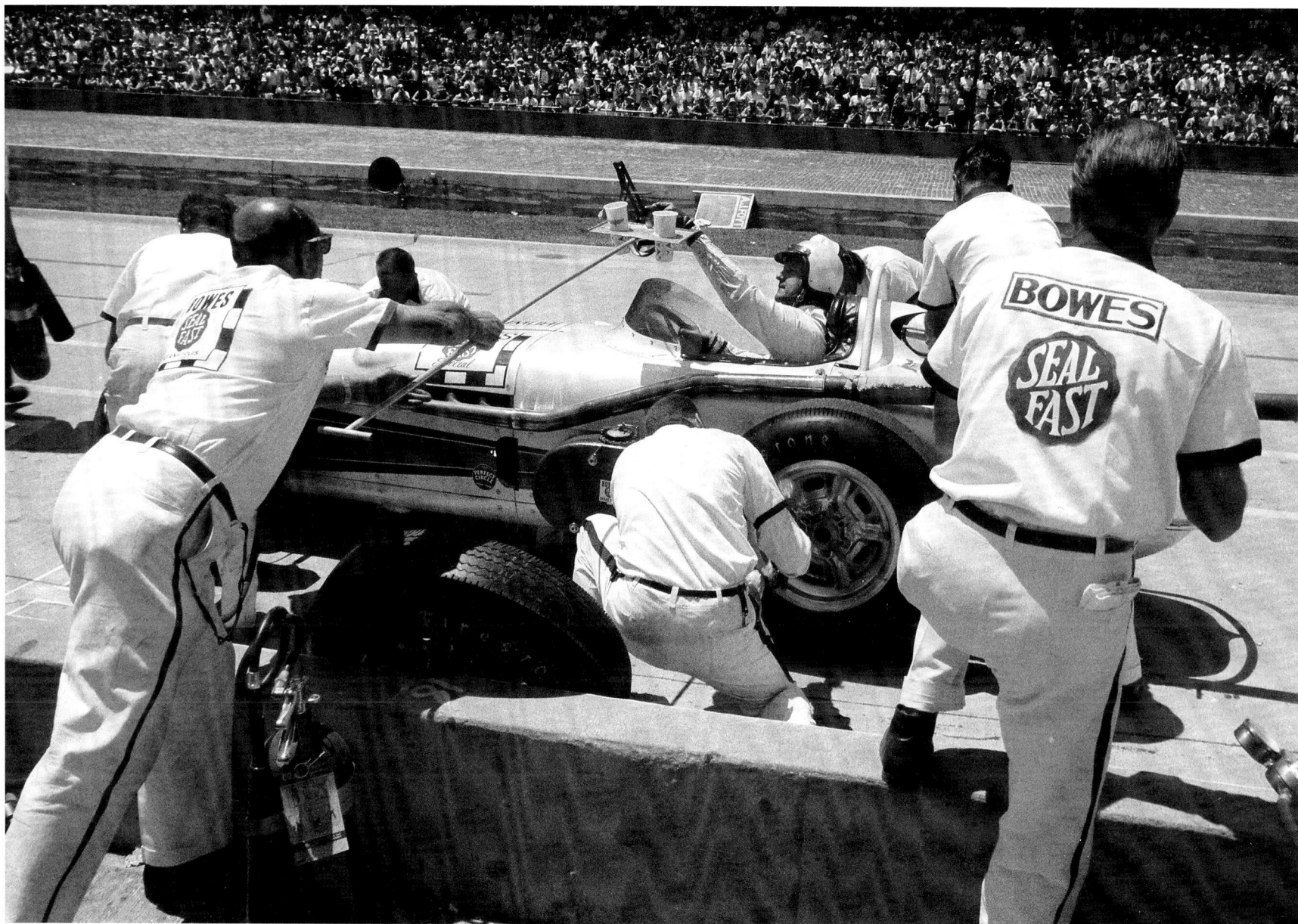

A. J. Foyt making his final pit stop on route to his first win at Indianapolis in 1961. Note that the front straightaway was still paved with bricks. This was the last year of that tradition. In 1962 the entire track was paved except for a three foot section at the start-finish line.

A. J. Shepard makes a rather spectacular exit from the 1962 Hoosier Hundred. When seeing this photograph, Shepard replied "I didn't plan it this way, God, I am hell on fences."

Graham Hill at the wheel of a wedge-shaped STP-Lotus Turbocar that led the 1968 Indianapolis 500, with Joe Leonard driving, until a minor problem caused it to retire nine laps from the finish.

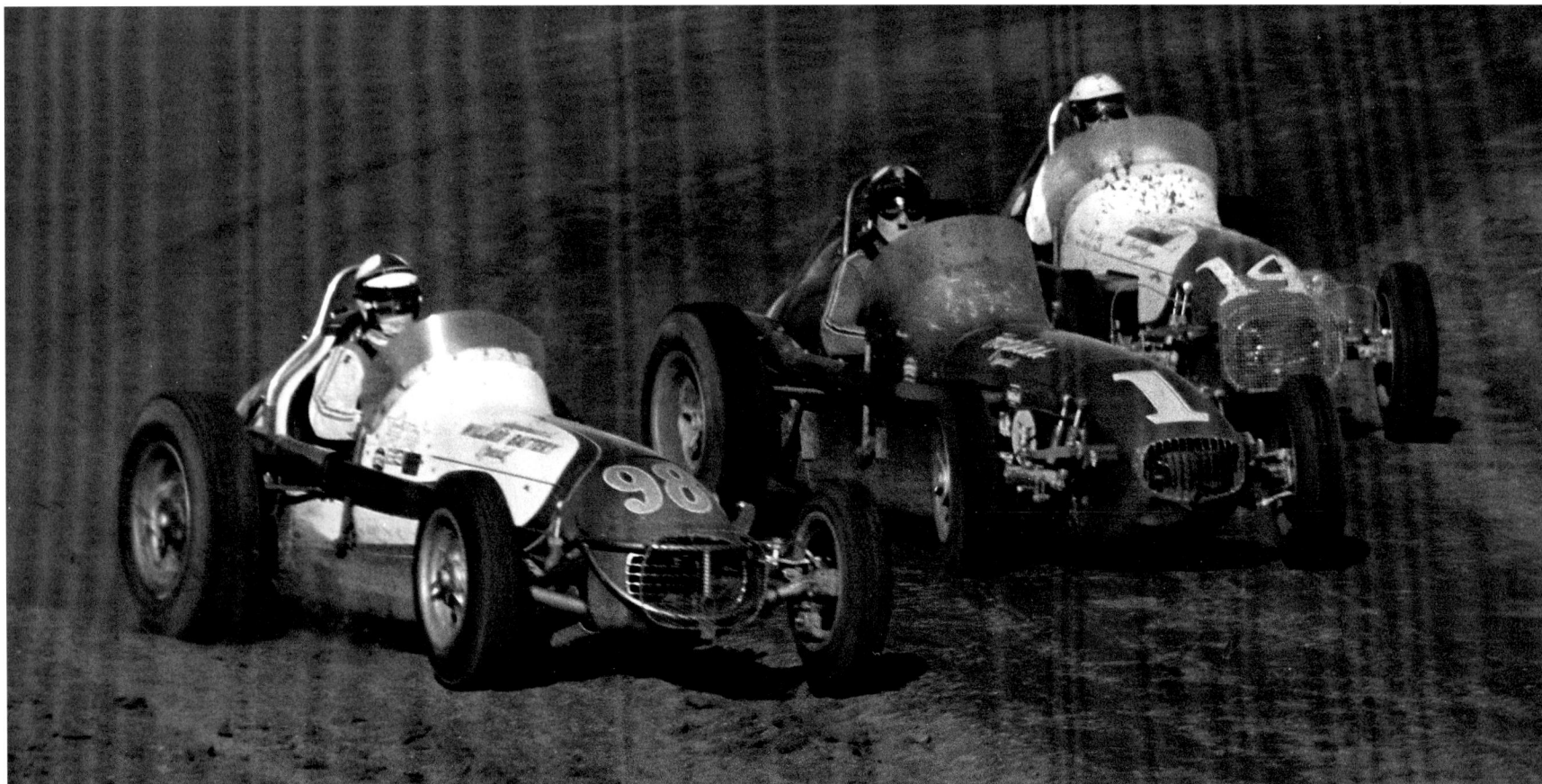

One of the closest dirt car races of the early 1960's took place at Phoenix in November, 1962. Parnelli Jones (98), Bobby Marshman (1), and A.J. Foyt (14) raced wheel to wheel for 50 laps. Marshman won his only championship race that day over Foyt and Jones.

Jim Hurtubise, flat out at Sacramento in November, 1960.

Len Sutton spins during the 1961 Indianapolis 500 as Ebb Rose (86) and another driver pass by.

The incredible 700 horsepower, supercharged, Novi V8 engine ready to run. Anyone who ever heard it run will never forget it.

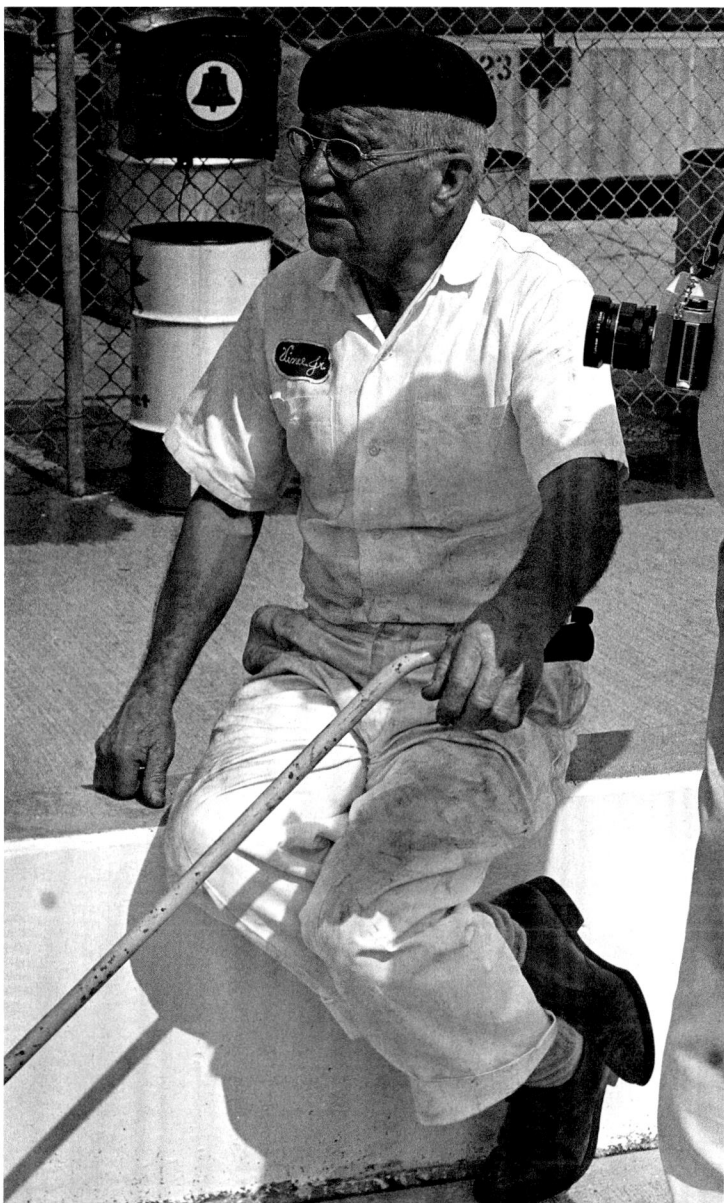

Jean Marcenac's name is synonymous with the Novi. He was responsible for the years of preparation that went into making the Novi the legend that it was.

Ryan Falconer rebuilding one of the Novi engines prior to the 1964 Indianapolis 500.

Greg Weld drove the Novi in its final appearance at Indianapolis in 1966. Weld crashed the car and it did not qualify.

Art Malone in the Kurtis-Novi. Of the three Novis qualified for the 1964 Indianapolis 500, Malone had the highest finish at eleventh.

Jim Hurtubise gave Novi fans one of their last great thrills when he took the lead from Parnelli Jones and led the first lap of the 1963 Indianapolis 500.

A.J. Foyt—Winner—Indianapolis 500, 1961, 1964, 1967, 1977.

Rodger Ward—Winner—Indianapolis 500, 1959, 1962.

Bobby Unser—Winner—Indianapolis 500, 1968, 1975, 1981.

Teammates Dan Gurney and Jim Clark congratulate each other after finishing seventh and second at the 1963 Indianapolis 500.

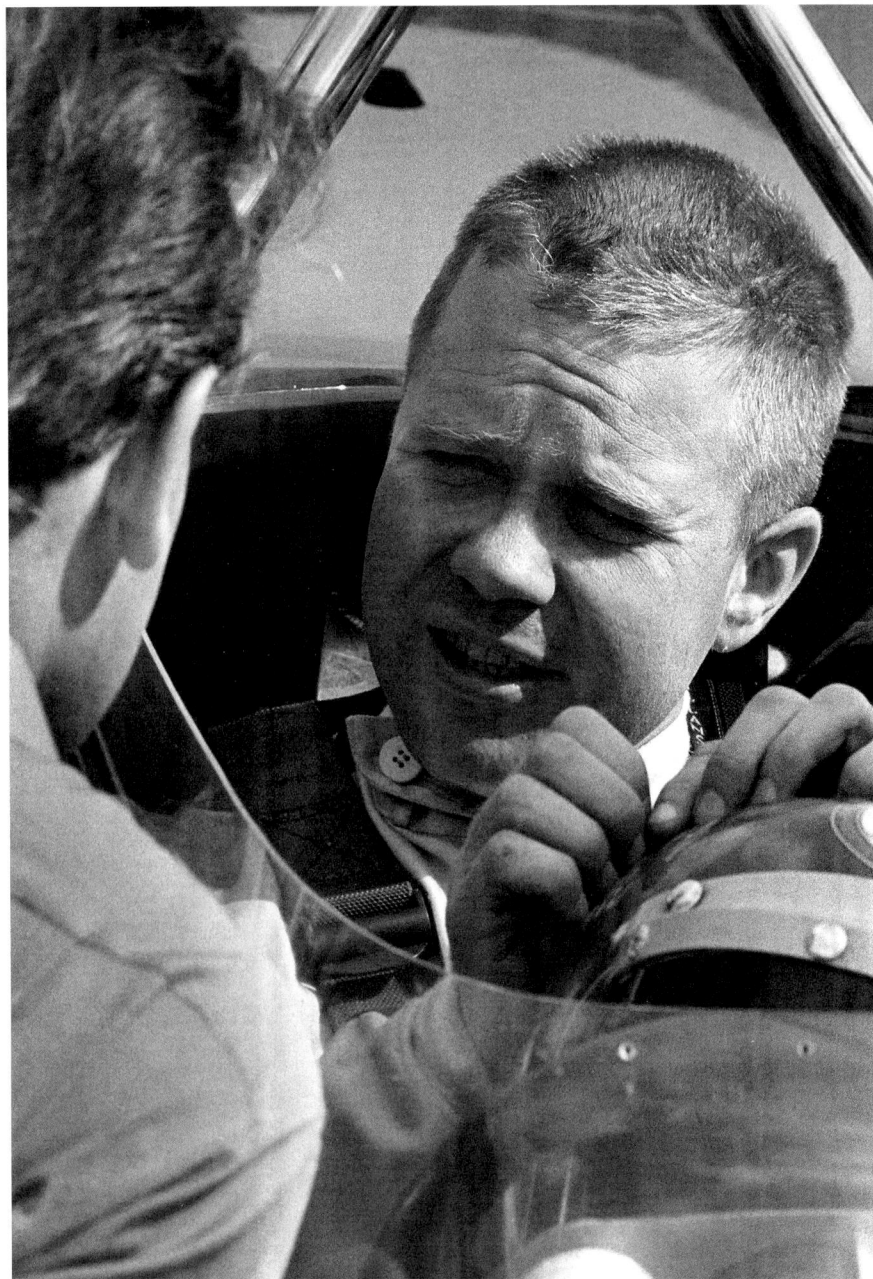

1969 Indianapolis Rookie of the Year, Mark Donohue talks to Lola designer Eric Broadley.
This was the first year that the Penske team came to the speedway.

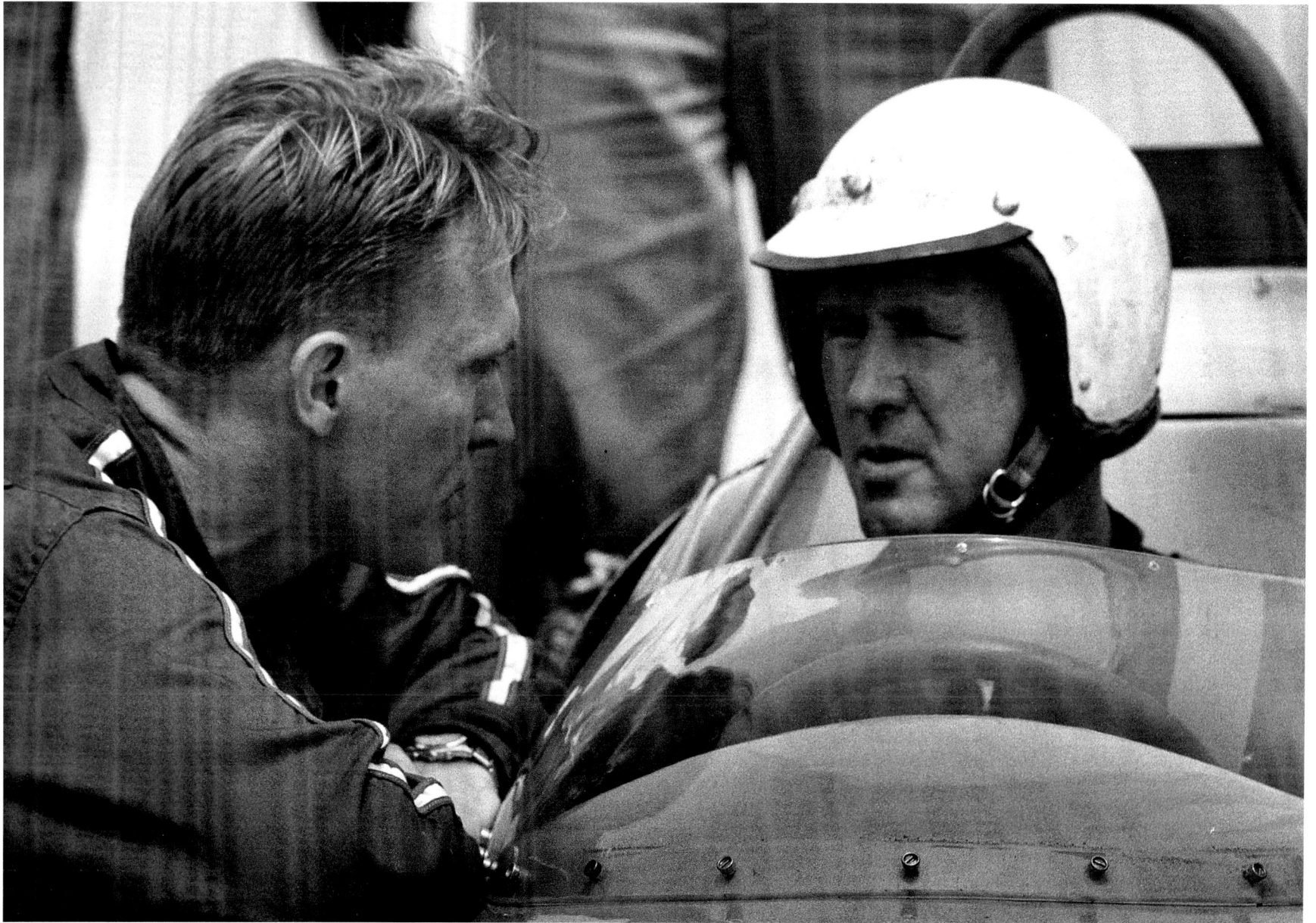

Rookie Dan Gurney seeks advice from veteran driver Duane Carter during practice for the 1962 Indianapolis 500.

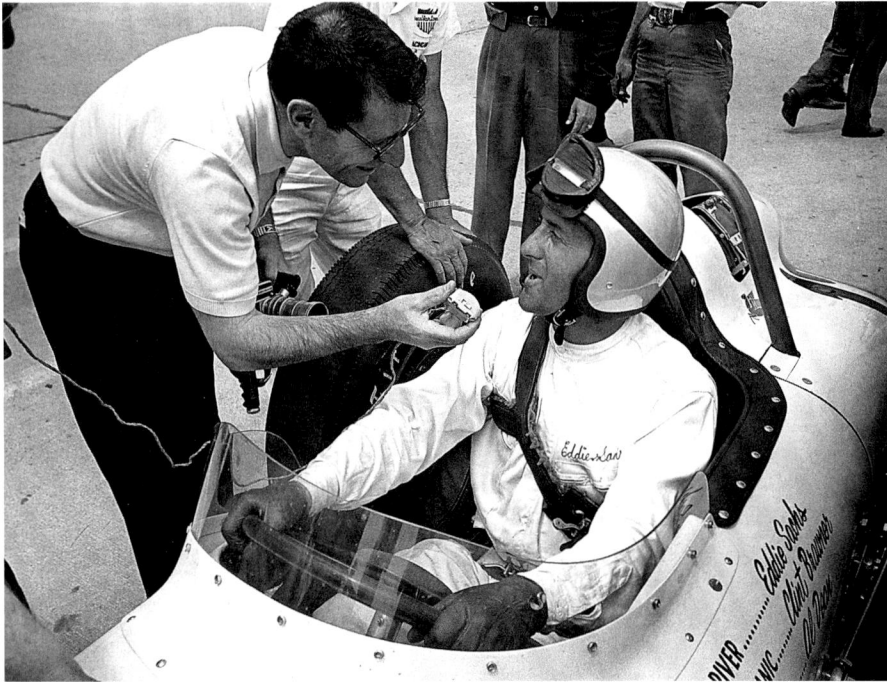

Eddie Sachs, never at a loss for words, is interviewed after qualifying for the 1961 Indianapolis 500.

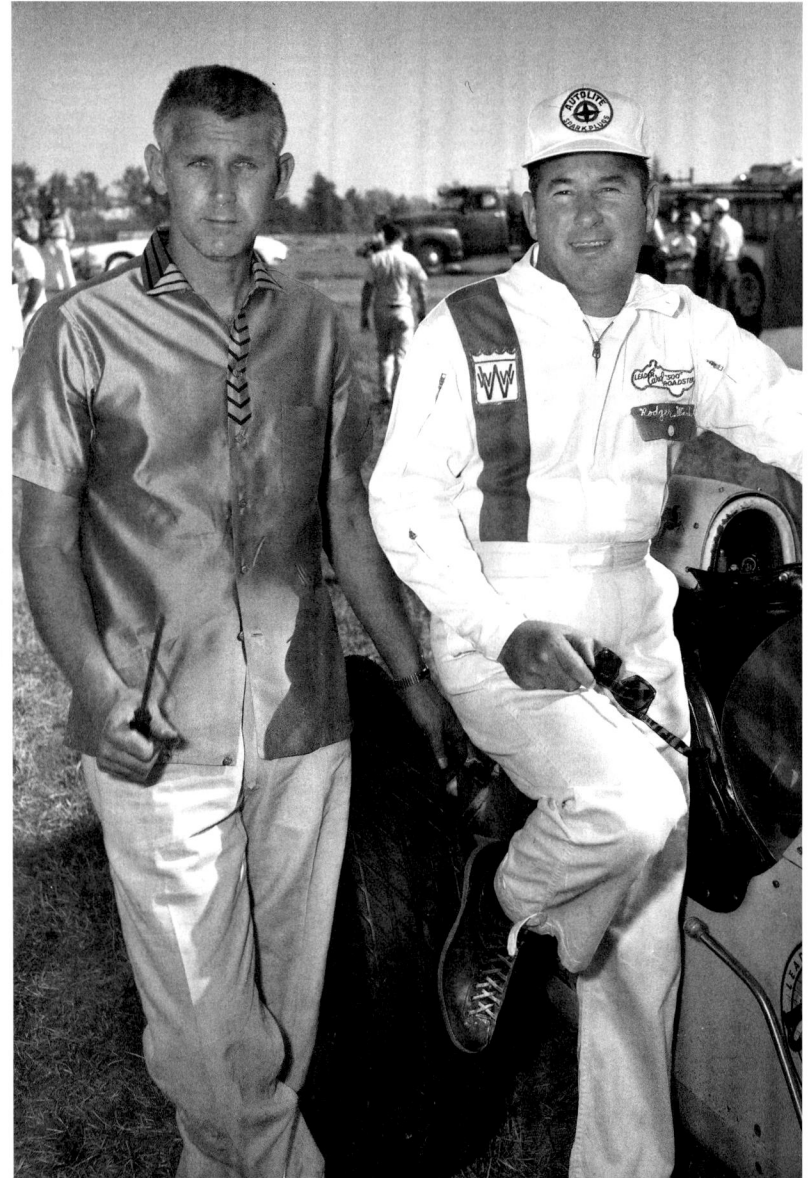

A.J. Watson and Rodger Ward formed another of the very successful driver-mechanic teams of the 1960's.

Parnelli Jones, Andy Granatelli, and Joe Leonard celebrate Leonard's pole position and new track record at the 1968 Indianapolis 500.

Jackie Stewart and team owner John Mecom switch hats during a break in practice at the 1966 Indianapolis 500.

These two Scottish drivers represent five world championships and one Indianapolis 500 win. Jackie Stewart and Jim Clark were not only fierce competitors — they were good friends.